T0368746

THERE IS HOPE

And Other Lessons Learned
by a Christian Cop

CHRIS AMOS

WESTBOW
PRESS
A DIVISION OF THOMAS NELSON

WestBow Press books may be ordered through booksellers or by contacting:

WestBow Press
A Division of Thomas Nelson
1663 Liberty Drive
Bloomington, IN 47403
www.westbowpress.com
1-(866) 928-1240

ISBN: 978-1-4497-3489-3 (sc)
ISBN: 978-1-4497-3490-9 (hc)
ISBN: 978-1-4497-3488-6 (e)
Library of Congress Control Number: 2011962787

Printed in the United States of America

WestBow Press rev. date: 2/06/2012

DEDICATION

I would like to dedicate *There Is Hope* to my wife, Anne Marie; children Seth and his wife, Stacey; Jesse and his wife, Lydia; and Hannah Grace for their unconditional love and support. I have been blessed beyond measure as a husband and father. There is hope, and I get to see it every day in the eyes of my wife and children.

ACKNOWLEDGMENTS

I am greatly indebted to my wife, Anne Marie, for insisting that I resurrect this manuscript, blow off the dust, and get back to work completing what the Lord had begun many years earlier. I also am grateful to my friends of the Norfolk Police Department, especially my partner David Huffman for his unwavering support as I've attempted to walk my talk on the streets of Norfolk. Finally, I want to thank my mentors and members of my own Christian Mount Rushmore: Pastor Lamar Sentell, Chief Charlie Grant, Judge Hal Bonney, and Clyde Odom.

CONTENTS

INTRODUCTION
MEET THE STUDENT

I never was really good in school. I don't know; maybe I never really put the effort into it that was needed to do as well as my two older brothers, who both graduated with honors. I was happy enough just to graduate. My motto was always, "I'd take common sense over book sense anytime." Reading between the lines, I think I was really saying, "I'll take the easy way out."

Looking back, I see how I was as determined to take the easy way out in life as I had been in school. The result was a life spent trying to avoid learning the first lesson God had in store for me—a lesson that took twenty-four years before I finally claimed it as mine.

Being the third of six kids, four boys and two girls, I found myself playing the role of peacemaker early in life. Somebody had better be able to keep the peace when Mom and Dad weren't around. That somebody was me.

I was raised in a Christian home and knew, or so I thought, everything I needed to know about God and Jesus Christ. Unfortunately, what little I did know never made it from my head to my heart. They say from the head to the heart is the longest twelve inches in the world. I'd have to agree. Don't get me wrong; head knowledge is good, but when the walls of life came crashing in—and those walls came crashing in early and often—I found my head knowledge of God to be of very little comfort.

The unraveling of my life began many years ago at the naive age of ten. Let me explain.

Have you ever explored forbidden territory or, like Eve, been offered forbidden fruit? Do you remember the sweaty palms, the racing heartbeat, the rush of adrenaline, the unbridled excitement and sense of expectancy? It was that rush that led this ten-year-old boy into his neighbor Skip's backyard. My sights were set on a large cluster of bushes, neatly tucked away in the corner of the yard. *What if someone sees you? What if their dog is loose? What if you're caught?* "What if" after "what if," my thoughts attempted to discourage my intentions, but to no avail; I had made up my mind, and nothing would stop me. I was going to reach that cluster of bushes—no ifs, ands, or buts.

Oh, it wasn't a tree of knowledge as was the case with Eve, but the pull, the desire, and the need to have what was contained within those bushes was just as real, just as controlling, just as mesmerizing. I quickly climbed the chain-link fence before sprinting across the yard and diving headfirst into the cluster of bushes, quickly disappearing into a sea of green leaves.

Once safely inside, my heart nearly burst as I began to dig in the dirt. *Oh no! It's gone!* I thought as I frantically began to dig deeper. My heart sank as I turned to leave, when suddenly, out of the corner of my eye, I saw something lying on the ground, placed neatly under a nearby bush. To this day I vividly remember my excitement as I quietly "thanked God" for this discovery. To be spiritually blind is to be *spiritually blind!*

I quickly reached for the folded package. Once it was in my hands, I carefully began to remove the plastic wrap that had protected this most prized possession from the inclement weather. I set the plastic wrap aside before carefully unfolding the hidden treasure.

There, on the cover, was a woman who seemed to scream out in a voice that only my hormones could hear, "I'm all yours!" Within seconds I was spellbound, gazing over glossy picture after picture of the most beautiful women in the world, at least as far as a ten-year-old kid with acne, a big nose, and warts was concerned. There they were, baring all just for me. The sting of being ridiculed and rejected, the big-nose jokes, the pizza-face insults—none of that mattered as I looked into the eyes of one beautiful woman after another who, strangely, seemed to accept me just as I was. I leafed through the magazine for several minutes before carefully and meticulously wrapping it back up in the plastic and tucking it back under the bush for future use. In the distance, no doubt the forces of hell were beginning to shout and scream in delight as the foundation was laid for a satanic stronghold that, in time, would come within inches of taking the life of its ten-year-old victim.

I wish a thousand times that I had walked away from that cluster of bushes never to return, but wishes, like talk, are cheap. The fact is, I did return to my forbidden fruit several more times before deciding that rather than risk being caught, it made more sense to take my hidden treasure home. And so I did, beginning a secretive fourteen-year addiction to pornography that was devastating.

Eventually that one magazine lost a bit of its luster, so I was compelled to seek out other sources of pornography. I discovered my friend Ronnie's father collected pornographic magazines, and shortly thereafter, Ronnie became my best friend. *Am I lucky or what?* I thought as I began to take advantage of this newfound goldmine of porn. Then there was the day I was walking down the street when there, lying on the ground right in front of me, was, you guessed it, a pornographic magazine. *I must be the luckiest guy in the world,* I thought. The tragedy of spiritual blindness is that what I saw as luck and good fortune was nothing more than the tragic formation of a satanic stronghold that would imprison me for years to come.

Throughout this time, I managed to keep my addiction a secret from everyone, family and friends alike. You might ask, "What do you mean, *addiction?* How can someone be addicted to pornography?" I was addicted in the sense that I would be overcome with mental cravings for porn at all hours of the day or night. Once overcome, I would do whatever it took to quench that craving. At times it was as easy as looking through a magazine I may have had hidden in my bedroom. If that wasn't possible, I would head to a local bookstore and browse through their magazines. And I always had the goldmine at my best friend's house.

Over the course of a few years, Satan managed to use porn as a sort of wedge, driving it deeper and deeper into my life. Unknowingly, through porn, I was slowly being isolated from my friends, church, family, and eventually God Himself. Oh, I was still physically very much an active part of these groups, but mentally and emotionally I was often very much alone. Once isolated, I was easily controlled, influenced, and in fact, driven by pornographic temptations and urges.

This isolation led to a level of depression and despair that I was able to soothe only by slipping away into a make-believe fantasy world provided through pornography. You see, it was in pornography that I found acceptance, power, control, and, dare I say, love—four things a boy with very low self-esteem and little self-worth would need desperately. What a horrific cycle of devastation I found myself trapped in, unwilling or unable (or perhaps a little of both) to get out of it.

As the years went by, I continually sought ways to escape this destructive cycle. Maybe, just maybe, I would find relief with a girlfriend. Then I'd be able to overcome my pornographic cravings. At the age of eighteen, I had my first and only girlfriend, Anne Marie. I was wrong; my addiction raged on unabated. Okay, my plan B was that I counted on marriage to bring relief; none came. After marrying Anne Marie at the age of twenty, I still found myself very much addicted. In fact, my addiction became even worse, as did the desperation and sense of hopelessness I experienced. Now I was not only deceiving my family and friends, but living a lie in front of my precious wife, who knew nothing of the pornographic stronghold that imprisoned me. Moving right along to plan C, I hoped the answer I so desperately sought would come by way of a baby.

I had gone through my life appearing to be an easygoing, happy, go-with-the-flow kind of guy, when truthfully I was dying a slow death. Living this kind of double life forced me to deceive my wife, my family, and my friends. Although I did not enjoy doing so, I was able to live with it and continue functioning. That ability to deceive and continue on as if nothing had ever happened came to a grinding halt the evening Seth was born. *You are a father now, Chris. It is time you get control of yourself,* I reminded myself in the days after Seth's birth. Something very strange began to happen in my life during this time.

The pornographic cravings, suddenly and without warning, stopped. I was on cloud nine as I found myself relishing my newfound role as a father. Life was finally going to take a turn for the better. My lust for porn was replaced by an overwhelming love for my newborn son. The nightmare that had been my addiction to pornography was finally coming to an end, or so I thought.

Within a couple of weeks, my hope of a new life free from porn came to a tragic end. Without understanding why, I found myself frequenting the same adult bookstores and go-go bars of my past. Like a moth to the flame, I found myself walking back into these poorly lit, smoke-filled dens of despair and depression. Like a house of cards caught by a passing gust of wind, I crumbled within. With my newfound hope shattered, I looked into the precious, innocent eyes of my own flesh-and-blood baby boy and realized I could not, would not, go on living the way I had been. Having run out of options, I was left with one last plan—plan D: *suicide*.

LESSON 1
THERE IS HOPE

Now may the God of hope fill you with all joy and peace in believing, that you may abound in hope by the power of the Holy Spirit.

—Romans 15:13

Sitting on the end of my bed, I watched my reflection in the mirror as I slowly began to raise the loaded .38 revolver to my head. First placing the gun inside my mouth and then moving it just above my right ear, I began to squeeze the trigger, ready to end all the hidden pain and suffering that had become the norm in my life. Oh, I knew suicide was the permanent solution to a temporary problem. But friend, when you get to a point of such despair and pain, you will eagerly embrace *any* solution.

Looking back I see how Satan had done his homework well, preparing me for this moment. At the age of twenty-one, I had graduated from the Norfolk Police Academy. Now, at twenty-four, I was ready to take my life and had the means to do so. Satan had made good use of my time on the department. The sights and sounds of death had become an almost daily routine. I found myself responding to far too many murders, shootings, stabbings, and suicides to count. In fact in the weeks leading up to the decision to end my life, I had been inundated with death, particularly suicides.

I thought of the eighteen-year-old man who slipped into his bathroom during a surprise birthday party thrown in his honor. A day of celebration without warning soon turned into an evening of tragedy. The police were called to the scene after his girlfriend was unable to get him to open the bathroom door. I heard the gunshot as I was entering the apartment. Forcing the bathroom door open, I saw this young man curled up, lying lifeless on the tile floor, a steady stream of blood continuing to flow from the side of his head. While standing over this eighteen-year-old's body, thinking, *That doesn't look so bad,* the seed of suicide had been cleverly planted.

In the weeks that followed, I helped lower a man who had hanged himself, assisted paramedics with restraining a college student who had slit her wrists, helped funeral home personnel lift the body of a man murdered, and protected the bloody crime scene where yet another man had been beaten to death. Unbeknownst to me, I was becoming totally desensitized to the value of life, whether that of another or my own.

Looking back, I had it all: a beautiful wife and son, excellent health, a great job, true friends, a loving church, and a nice home. I appeared to have the world by the tail, but appearances can be deceiving. Well hidden from my wife and son, hidden from my family and friends, hidden from everyone was a life-destroying addiction to pornography. I had spent the better part of my life, fourteen of twenty-four years, living a lie: hiding behind masks that on the outside portrayed an easygoing, levelheaded guy with a PhD in common sense. Ever the optimist, I had the admiration and respect of family and friends alike, loving life on the outside while dying a slow and painful death within.

Finally, the time had come to do the very thing I had seen so many others do: commit suicide. The reasons vary with each person, but at the heart of most, I would say, is an overwhelming, all-consuming, life-destroying sense of utter hopelessness. *Go ahead, Chris, do yourself a favor. It's best for Anne Marie and Seth. They deserve better.* Wave after wave of suicidal thoughts flooded my mind with a relentlessness that in time eroded any desire I may have had to resist.

Watching myself in the mirror, looking into the eyes of one who had lost all hope, knowing Anne Marie had taken Seth and would not be home for several hours, I knew today was the day to end the pain and suffering I had grown so very tired of. My hand was unusually steady and my breathing was calm and measured as I placed the barrel inside my mouth before removing it and pressing it against my head. With one final, deep breath I began to squeeze the trigger, watching the hammer on my department-issued .38 revolver as it began to move backward. Within a fraction of an inch from eternity it happened. The unthinkable, the unimaginable, the unbelievable happened. Simply put, God showed up. I mean, out of nowhere, as I was a fraction of an inch from eternity and hell, I heard an audible voice. A voice more powerful than any I had ever heard. The voice lovingly yet forcefully said, "There is hope." Those three words were like an atomic bomb shattering every thought of hopelessness, despair, and suicide that had taken a stranglehold on my mind, fourteen years in the making. Those three heaven-sent words were enough to cause me to release the trigger and begin to lower my gun.

Startled, I instinctively began to look under the bed and in the bathroom in search of the voice's source. I put the gun back into my holster, dumbfounded at what had just occurred and yet sensing, for the first time, that there truly was hope. This was the beginning of a six-month journey that ultimately led me to hope incarnate, Jesus Christ.

In *There Is Hope* I share a number of life-changing lessons I have learned in the months and years since that 1989 August day: lessons that I pray may shed the light of God's life-transforming hope and grace into the lives of men and women, young and old, who like me desperately need to hear those precious lifesaving words, "There is hope!"

Just as surely as Satan is the creator of hopelessness and despair, so too is Jesus Christ the creator, source, and very essence of hope. To those contemplating suicide I say the pain, anger, despair, loneliness, rejection, and hopelessness you feel is real. It is not a figment of your imagination. It is not simply a clinical diagnosis attributed to stress, to be treated with medication. It is real and it is devastating. But, I must also say, so is the unquenchable hope found in Jesus Christ. To that man, woman, or teenager ready to end it all, I shout from the very depths of my heart, soul, mind, and strength, "There is hope!"

Lesson 1: There is hope! I know ... I saw it in the mirror this morning.

LESSON 2
LIFE IS LIKE A MIST

Come now, you who say, "Today or tomorrow we will go to such and such a city, spend a year there, buy and sell, and make a profit"; whereas you do not know what will happen tomorrow. For what *is* your life? It is even a vapor that appears for a little time and then vanishes away.

—James 4:13–14

"Gunshot victim on the corner of Smith and State," the dispatcher broadcasted.

"One-four-three to radio," I responded. "Put me on an assist on Smith."

As I arrived, dusk was falling quickly and units were already on the scene looking for but unable to find a victim. Most of the police and rescue units on the scene had cleared when I heard a soft-spoken voice coming from the back door of an old, dilapidated rooming house.

"He's over here," a voice said softly from behind an old, faded white wooden door desperately in need of a fresh coat of paint. I ran to the back door and began to push, but the door didn't budge. As I pushed harder, the door began to slowly give way. As it opened, I noticed something glistening down by my feet. I looked down and saw that I was standing in a pool of blood. I made one final push before the door opened and I entered.

"One-four-three to radio," I called urgently.

"One-four-three, go ahead," the dispatcher responded.

"I've located the victim."

I turned to the elderly woman who had first gotten my attention and asked her the address of our location. I passed that information on to the dispatcher.

"What is the condition of the victim?" asked the dispatcher.

"It looks like he has at least one gunshot wound to the head. He has a pulse, but it's weak. You better get rescue here ASAP."

This man would die in the back of an ambulance on the way to the hospital, becoming just another homicide statistic for that year. I later learned that the man responsible for his death was the victim's friend and roommate. Apparently the two had gotten into an argument over five dollars. Their verbal exchange quickly escalated to the use of a gun. Both men had been drinking.

As I stood on the blood-soaked kitchen floor, I noticed a plate of food on the table. Steam was still rising from the mashed potatoes and peas on the plate. Ironically, Larry, the victim, had sat down to eat dinner like he had done thousands of times before, only that night would not end like those in the past. Larry's plans were suddenly and violently interrupted, not just for that one night but for all of eternity.

Life is so uncertain, I thought, as the steam rose into the kitchen air before vanishing. *It is here, and then without warning, it's gone … just that quickly.*

Lesson 2: To plan for tomorrow means very little unless one has planned for eternity first. Tomorrow is guaranteed to none, eternity is to all.

LESSON 3
THE KINGDOM OF GOD

But Jesus said to them, "They do not need to go away.
You give them something to eat." And they said to Him,
"We have here only five loaves and two fish."

—Matthew 14:16–17

"**H**ey, do you collect pennies?" I heard Scott ask as I bent down to pick up a penny lying in the parking lot. Scott was the maintenance supervisor at a small apartment complex where I did part-time security work.

"Scott, as a matter of fact, I do. But, there's a reason behind it," I answered. "The Bible describes an event in which Jesus multiplied a few fish and a couple of loaves of bread to feed a crowd numbering in the thousands."

"Yeah, Chris, I'm familiar with the story, but what does that have to do with you collecting pennies?" he asked.

"I just figure that if Jesus can multiply fish and bread to meet the needs of people, then he can do the same with a penny to meet the needs of His church. Besides, every time I pick one up, God reminds me that I'm in the kingdom-building business."

"Wait here a minute, Chris. I'll be right back," Scott said as he turned to walk away.

A few minutes passed, and then suddenly Scott reappeared carrying two large jars of pennies, one under each arm. "Here," he said as he handed me the two jars, "take these."

"What are they for?" I asked, a little bewildered.

"The kingdom of God," he replied, smiling.

I thanked Scott for the pennies as I marveled at what God had done.

A few days later I felt the Holy Spirit prompting, "Chris, God has multiplied that one penny. Now you need to start counting and find out how many times."

I immediately stopped what I was doing, ran up to my room, and began the slow, tedious process of counting hundreds of pennies. The same God who had multiplied a handful of fish and a couple of loaves of bread had done the same with one penny. In fact He had multiplied that one penny 3,751 times!

Lesson 3: Little is much when God is in it.

LESSON 4
SOULS, NOT CENTS

But Jesus said to them, "They do not need to go away.
You give them something to eat." And they said to Him,
"We have here only five loaves and two fish."

—Matthew 4:19

My partner and I pulled up to the corner and immediately saw three
men standing together on the sidewalk in "Weed Alley." The
area got its name from the heavy concentration of marijuana dealers
and users who frequented that location. If you wanted to sell or buy
marijuana, Weed Alley was the place to go. As I stepped out of my car
and approached the men, I unknowingly stepped over a dollar bill that
was lying in the gutter. I had begun to ask the three men a few questions
when one of them saw the dollar and quickly moved to pick it up.

Over the previous several months I had made it a habit to pick up
any money, usually pennies, I saw lying on the ground. I give them to
build the kingdom of God. I couldn't help but think as I watched the
man push the dollar bill into his pocket that I had just blown the chance
of giving 100 pennies to help build the kingdom of God. I finished my
conversation with the three men before returning to my car somewhat
dejected over my missed opportunity to add to God's kingdom.

As the evening wore on, I couldn't shake the disappointment of not
seeing that dollar bill. After all, wouldn't that have made a tremendous

witness to the guys I was working with that night? I mean, it's just not an everyday occurrence to find a dollar on the ground. *Oh, well,* I thought, *what's done is done, Chris. It's water under the bridge now.*

Three hours later I found myself talking with Jeff, a cocaine addict who was desperately wanting to break free from an addiction that was destroying his life.

"Sir, I just can't escape," Jeff said. "I try and try and try, but it keeps pulling me back. I've tried NA [Narcotics Anonymous] and AA [Alcoholics Anonymous], but it just doesn't seem to work."

"Jeff," I responded, "what you need is Jesus Christ. What you are fighting is far more powerful than NA and AA and every other self-help support group. Unfortunately, many of these groups treat symptoms and never get to the root source. Jesus and Jesus alone can remove that source. No one or nothing else can."

Jeff took a deep breath before saying, "I'm withering away, sir. I'll try anything."

"Jeff, are you serious about getting help?" I asked.

By this time tears had begun to form in this grown man's eyes— eyes that seemed to cry out for help and hope.

"Yes, sir, I am serious. If Jesus can help me, I want His help. I need His help"—a long pause followed—"before it's too late."

Jeff gave me his phone number and address, and to my utter disbelief I discovered that he and I lived in the same neighborhood. I quietly thanked God for this "miracle" before asking Jeff one last question.

"If you really want help, then I will give you a call sometime this week, okay?"

Jeff looked into my eyes as tears began to trickle down his face. "Sir, I have been waiting for this to happen for a long time. Yes, please call me. I need help." We shook hands before parting ways.

As I left the station late that night, I was reminded of the dollar bill I had failed to see. Suddenly, I sensed the voice of God saying, "Chris, the dollar you didn't see means nothing to me. I know your motives are pure, but I do not need the pennies or the occasional dollar you find to build my kingdom. The pennies you find and pick up for my kingdom are not for me but for you. What I mean is that every time you pick up a penny, I am reminding you that you are a kingdom builder. Yet you must understand that my kingdom is not made of dollars and cents. My kingdom is made of people just like you who have accepted my Son as their Savior and Lord. Tonight you missed an opportunity to add a dollar to the kingdom of God, but in its place you have been given an opportunity to share my message of love, forgiveness, and hope to a man desperately lost in sin. Chris, I would rather have one Jeff added to my kingdom than a million dollars. Please remember this the next time you find a penny, and may it remind you that the pennies you find are not your gift to me, but rather mine to you. Build on, Chris, build on."

I passed Jeff's house that night on the way home, and as I did, I understood for the first time what it really meant to be a kingdom builder.

Lesson 4: The kingdom we are called to help build is made of souls, not cents.

LESSON 5
WHEN TRAGEDY HITS HOME

Blessed be the God and Father of our Lord Jesus Christ, the
Father of mercies and God of all comfort, who comforts us
in all our tribulation, that we may be able to comfort those
who are in any trouble, with the comfort with which we
ourselves are comforted by God.

—2 Corinthians 1:3–4

As a police officer the thought of a person committing suicide, though
disturbing, becomes almost routine. I have seen the aftermath of
this tragedy more times than I care to remember. I have been in the
unenviable position of having to comfort those whose worlds have been
rocked and whose lives have been shattered by the suicide of a loved one
or friend. Little did I know that I was about to respond to a suicide that
would not only rock my world but turn it completely upside down.

The note was short enough, the words were few, and yet the effect
of that note has left an incredible impression on my life. The note simply
said, "CFA card is in my wallet. Papers are in desk. Can never get well
and can't stand pain. Love, Cyril." The note was written by an elderly
man just minutes before he walked into his bathroom, held a gun to his
head, and pulled the trigger. His hands were obviously shaking as he
put to paper his final thoughts. So, too, were mine as I read those final
pain-riddled thoughts ... of my grandfather.

That Friday afternoon was passing as had so many in the past. I was getting dressed for work when my wife came rushing into the room. "Chris, something has happened to Gramps. He's been rushed to the hospital."

I began asking questions she could not answer. Within a few minutes I was on the phone with my uncle who was at the hospital with Gramps.

"Jerry, what happened?" I asked. *Surely Gramps had a stroke or heart attack,* I thought. After all, he had been having some pretty rough bouts with his health.

"Chris," Jerry answered, his voice cracking, "your grandfather shot himself."

I sat motionless on my bed. *No, no,* I thought, *this can't be. Suicide is something that happens to other people and other families.* I knew. I had seen it happen to other people over and over again.

Jerry wasn't finished. "Chris, your grandfather is dead."

The impact of those words, "your grandfather is dead," did not hit home until several days later. I hung up with Jerry and told my wife the news before rushing over to my grandparents' house. I spent the next few hours side by side with my brother and dad, cleaning up the bathroom in which Gramps shot himself.

Not wanting to believe what had happened and yet unable to deny it, we went about mopping up pools of blood that had formed on the tile bathroom floor. *Something is terribly wrong,* I thought. *I've never had to do this before. I have always handled suicides professionally, filling out the proper reports, making the necessary phone calls, and comforting those left behind as best as possible before quietly walking away.*

This was different. I was not the consoling police officer. No, this time I was the bewildered loved one not really knowing what to say or how to say it. I became sick to my stomach as I realized there would be no walking away this time.

In the weeks that followed Gramp's death, a strange thing began to happen to me. The pain and anger I had felt in the immediate aftermath of his suicide slowly began to give way to something illogical, something irrational, something truly astonishing. It was as if God had given me a tremendous peace concerning Gramps, and a newfound capacity to love and sympathize with others who had been touched by the tragic suicide of a family member or friend.

For the first time in my life I could not only complete the proper reports and make the necessary phone calls but was able to comfort those left behind, with the very comfort God had given me. I could say with all truthfulness and sincerity, "By the grace of God you will get through this. It will be hard; it will even seem impossible at times. The pain may feel inconsolable, the loss too great to ever move beyond. But you can and you will get through this."

I know I did.

Lesson 5: God may very well use the pain we experience today to produce hope for someone else tomorrow.

LESSON 6

"WILL YOU HUG ME?"

Beloved, let us love one another, for love is of God; and everyone who loves is born of God and knows God. He who does not love does not know God, for God is love. In this the love of God was manifested toward us, that God has sent His only begotten Son into the world, that we might live through Him. In this is love, not that we loved God, but that He loved us and sent His Son to be the propitiation for our sins. Beloved, if God so loved us, we also ought to love one another.

—1 John 4:7–11

I will never forget the desperate look in the young boy's eyes as he lifted his arms toward me and asked, "Will you hug me?" I bent down to pick up the six-year-old, and my heart began to break as he firmly wrapped his arms around my neck, not wanting to let go.

The boy's name was Joey. He and his eight-year-old sister, Jenny, had been left at home alone while their grandmother was at work. A concerned neighbor called the police, and I arrived to investigate. Over the next hour and a half the pieces of a heartbreaking yet all-too-familiar puzzle began to fall into place.

I arrived at the address only to find an apartment that was locked and appeared unoccupied. The neighbor came out and assured me two young children were alone inside and had been all day. I returned to the apartment and began to call out, through a small mail slot in the door, to the kids inside. After continuing this for several minutes I saw a small head inside the apartment peek around a corner.

I encouraged her, "It's okay, honey—you're not in trouble. I'm here to help you; please open the door." She began to move cautiously toward the door.

As tears streamed down her face, the frightened child unlocked the door, and I entered. The apartment was modestly furnished. The floors were clean, the refrigerator and pantry were well stocked, and the air conditioner was working. The apartment looked almost homey with one exception: there was no mother or father or grandmother or any adult at all inside. Jenny and Joey were all alone and had been not just that day, but the previous two weeks. They lived with their grandma, who worked from 7:00 a.m. to 3:00 p.m., six days a week.

Grandma's rules were simple. Do not open the door for anyone or else you will be punished. Made perfectly good sense to me. Grandma also required both Joey and Jenny to clean up after themselves, which, again, would not be considered unreasonable. I must admit the kids were very well behaved, seemed responsible, and were very protective of each other, but as I won their trust, I began to see two young children who through circumstances beyond their control were being robbed of their childhood.

You see, as the other six- and eight-year-olds were riding bikes and playing ball, Jenny and Joey were washing dishes, vacuuming, dusting, ironing clothes, and preparing meals. The more we talked, the more childlike the kids became. It was as if something told them, "It's okay. This man will take care of you. He will protect you. You can be a little girl and little boy again."

I asked, "Jenny, where is your mommy?"

She replied, "My mommy lives in a different place."

"Where is your daddy?"

"We don't have a daddy."

"Why aren't you living with your mommy?"

"My mommy has too many babies in her house, so she sent us to live with Grandma."

I later learned that Jenny's mother was living in another low-income housing area in an apartment with seven small children. Jenny and Joey were living with Grandma because their mother could not handle raising nine kids. Grandma was forced to go back to work to help her daughter support her nine grandchildren. Thank God for grandmas!

I eventually turned the kids over to a social services worker who in turn was going to help the grandmother find an inexpensive day care center for Jenny and Joey. I realize nothing can take the place of a mother and a father, but at least while at day care, they may be able to act more like young children and less like miniature adults.

As I left that call, the words of an innocent six-year-old child once again shot through my mind like a knife through my heart: "Will you hug me?"

Lesson 6: God desires to hug a desperate, hurting world through the arms of His children.

LESSON 7
DOING THE RIGHT THING

For who is greater, he who sits at the table, or he who serves? Is it not he who sits at the table? Yet I am among you as the One who serves.

—Luke 22:27

"Excuse me, I think I just hit a dog with my car. The dog limped off toward that building," a visibly shaken woman said as she pointed toward City Hall. My partner and I thanked the woman before riding toward City Hall in search of the injured canine. Within a couple of minutes we were standing over a dead dog.

"Oh well," my partner said. "I'll call street cleaning." I nodded in agreement. We stood by the dead dog for almost an hour as we waited on street cleaning to respond. Little did we know that throughout this time we were being watched.

"Men," a deep voice behind us boomed out, "I've been watching you! As a small boy I was once told that there was a difference between doing what's right and doing the right thing. I just want you to know you have done the right thing today."

My partner and I looked at each other not really knowing how to take this gentleman who, for whatever reason, had spent the past hour of his life watching us stand next to a dead dog. "Thanks … I guess," I said as the man smiled before walking away.

21

Two months later Dave and I found ourselves voluntold to accompany our Lieutenant to the City's Class Act Awards luncheon. To our surprise we found ourselves recipients of one of the city's Class Act Awards for doing the "right thing" about the dead dog.

"You know, Dave, I could see getting this thing for pulling someone from a burning building or delivering a baby, but for—"

Before I could finish, Dave interrupted, "Tell me about it."

As the awards ceremony got under way I noticed two other recipients who no doubt had performed a feat equally as important as ours. The comfort I had in this thought was short lived as a letter of commendation was read describing the class act done by our fellow recipients.

"On the eighth of June," a high-ranking city official read, "Bob Jackson and Tim Richards saved the life of coworker Dan Adams. Bob and Tim discovered their coworker unconscious and immediately began performing CPR ..."

My heart began to race as Dave and I both began to look for the exit.

"Dave, do you get the idea we're at the wrong awards ceremony?" I whispered.

"Hey, saving a man's life or standing by a dead dog waiting for it to be hauled away. Six one way, half a dozen the other," Dave answered sarcastically.

"Lieutenant, how would you like to receive our award for us and we'll go ahead and get back to work?" I asked.

"I don't think so," he answered.

"Chris, we've been set up," Dave decided.

"What are you talking about?"

"Cameras, man, cameras. Allen Funk has got to be hiding around here someplace."

While still looking for Allen, the letter of commendation was finished and much-deserved Class Act Awards were given to Bob and Tim. An appreciative round of applause was given, hands were shaken, and then all eyes were turned toward two policemen who were now looking like fish out of water.

"Officers Amos and Huffman are to be commended for their actions on the twenty-second of June," the emcee read. You could feel the suspense grow. I mean, after all, we must have survived a deadly gun battle, foiled a bank robbery in progress, or saved a child from drowning in the city lake. The thoughts of heroism many may have had were quickly laid to rest as our letter of commendation continued to be read aloud. "These officers demonstrated the utmost in professionalism and compassion in the proper disposal of a dog that had been struck by a passing motorist ..."

At the conclusion of the letter Dave and I graciously received our Class Act Awards before quietly slipping out of the room. We hit the street wondering what Class Acts the day might hold.

Lesson 7: It's not the razzle-dazzle performance that makes a class act in the eyes of God, but devoted service during the ordinary, mundane routine of life.

LESSON 8
OOPS

And He spoke a parable to them: "Can the blind lead the blind? Will they not both fall into the ditch?"

—Luke 6:39

The phone lines downtown were flooded with calls from frightened neighbors, all reporting gunshots coming from a large house on Colonial Avenue. If one call comes in, no problem: a police officer checks it out. When five or six calls come in at once, all reporting the same thing, it's time to send the cavalry. Such was the case on that cool, clear evening in October.

"Radio to any units in the vicinity of the 6300 block of Colonial Avenue. We have multiple reports of shots being fired from 6308 Colonial Avenue."

Units immediately began to answer up.

"Unit one-three-six, put me on an assist on Colonial."

"Ten-four, one-three-six," the dispatcher acknowledged.

"One-three-four to radio, put myself and one-three-five on the message also."

"Ten-four, one-three-four. I'm showing one-three-four, three-five, and three-six all responding to Colonial. Is that everyone?" the dispatcher asked.

I answered up, "One three-three to radio, we are right around the corner. Put us on the assist also."

"I copied, one three-three. Be advised a K-9 unit is on the scene."

Our adrenaline began to flow as we headed toward Colonial Avenue. On the way we fell in line behind a couple of other units. The three of us raced toward Colonial with lights flashing and sirens blaring.

As we pulled up in front of 6308, I saw that a K-9 unit had already taken up a position directly in front of the suspect's house. The officer was using his truck for cover as he waited for backup. The four additional units that responded followed suit. We blocked off the street and then began to wait and watch for activity inside the house.

"One-three-six to one-three-zero," an officer on scene radioed.

"Go ahead," a supervisor answered.

"I'm going to try to make my way up to the front door to see if I can't get a better look inside the house, copy?"

"Okay, Mike. Do the other units know what you're up to?"

"Yeah, I've already told them."

By this time we had the house surrounded. My eyes strained as I watched the darkened outline of not just an officer but a friend make his way up to the front of a house whose occupants were reportedly armed and dangerous. You could have heard a pin drop as he made his way to the front door. The silence of the October night was suddenly broken.

"One-three-six to radio. What was the address the shots were coming from?" my friend asked as he illuminated the front door of the house with his flashlight.

"One-three-six, the address is 6308 Colonial Avenue," the dispatcher answered.

While still standing on the front porch, Mike turned toward the rest of us who were still safely hidden behind our police units. "Hey, guys, guess what? We've been watching the wrong house. This is 6309; 6308 is right behind you."

There was a collective groan as officers rushed around their cars in an effort to take cover from the right house this time. I've never seen so many police officers move so quickly.

After a few minutes we came to the consensus that if there was anyone inside 6308 Colonial Avenue with a gun, he would have had plenty of time to shoot all of us in the back. With that consensus reached, we decided to walk up to the door and knock. We did just that. Ten minutes later we left that house, leaving behind our shooter, a teenager, and his weapon, a BB gun. Fortunately for us we were dealing with a kid playing games and not a murderer looking to make the six o'clock news.

Lesson 8: In your Christian walk, don't assume the other person knows what he or she is doing. Read, study, and pray; your spiritual life depends on it.

LESSON 9
FAMILY

... not forsaking the assembling of ourselves together, as is the manner of some, but exhorting one another, and so much the more as you see the Day approaching.

—Hebrews 10:25

"To be perfectly honest, George," I said to a good friend from church and fellow police officer, "after this past week I feel like the sanitizing block in the bottom of a urinal."

George's only response was one of laughter as I continued. "I'm serious, man. I mean, the dirty jokes, the pessimism, the steady stream of profanity, the stories of sexual conquests—you name it, I've been around it this past week. It has a way of getting to you after a while."

George shook his head in agreement, knowing exactly what I was talking about. Not wanting to belabor my point but not really caring if I did, I continued, "It's like for a week I've been submerged in all this filth and this morning I came walking into church feeling dirty—or maybe *empty* is a better term."

"That explains Sunday school," George piped up.

Just an hour earlier I had stopped teaching my lesson after only about fifteen minutes. I confessed to the class that I had had a lousy week and that I had not prepared for the lesson like I should have.

"Folks, I was just telling Anne Marie on the way here that I had nothing to give. I mean, usually I come with a lesson that I know God has placed on my heart to share, but this morning it just wasn't there. I came, I started, I struggled, and now I confess. I feel like, this morning, I have nothing to offer, nothing to give, zippo, nada. You get the idea."

It really wasn't my intent to throw a pity party. It was my intent, however, to be transparent to my class. Within a couple of minutes different folks began to really lift me up, not in an arrogant or boastful way, but in Christian love. Their words of encouragement began to restore the hope and joy that had seemed to desert me the week before. I walked out of class knowing I was there not to give, but to receive the kind and appreciative words of my brothers and sisters in Christ.

I soon found myself kneeling at the altar during the morning service. I had closed my eyes and begun to pray when suddenly I felt someone's hand on my arm. I looked up only to see Kevin, another dear brother in Christ, who began to pray not simply with me but for me. I rose from that altar thankful for Kevin, George, Tom, Paul, and many of my Christian friends.

While sitting through the sermon I thought about what it had been like a few days earlier. "Oh, Father," I quietly prayed, "if only it were possible for me to become a professional, full-time church attendee, forty-plus hours a week, making a living going to church without having to leave the warmth and safety of your sanctuary. If only it were possible, Lord, but I know that is crazy. It's not in the warmth and safety of the sanctuary that you desire to save a dying world. Father, strengthen me for what lies ahead, and may I never forget that I have a church family that loves and supports me even when those in the world do not."

Lesson 9: To reject fellowship with a Christ-honoring church is to choose to live life as a spiritual orphan. Find a church family today!

LESSON 10
SUFFER NOW, CELEBRATE LATER

Listen, my beloved brethren: Has God not chosen the poor
of this world to be rich in faith and heirs of the kingdom
which He promised to those who love Him?

—James 2:5

Ms. Beulah was seventy-seven years old the night I first met her.
The circumstances of that initial meeting were not the most ideal.
Ms. Beulah had called the police to report a vandalism, and I was the
officer dispatched to her residence.

As I arrived at her apartment and began knocking on the door, I
quickly realized that whoever lived inside lived not only in one of the
most violent public housing complexes in the city, but, to make matters
worse, she lived in the very middle of the complex. After I had waited a
few minutes, the door cracked open and there stood an elderly woman
hunched over with a look of fear in her eyes. I identified myself as the
police, and the fear gave way to relief as she swung the door open and
invited me inside.

"Ma'am, are you alone?" I asked before entering her apartment.

"I've got my Jesus," she responded without hesitation.

Well, if it isn't safe with her Jesus, it isn't safe anywhere, I thought as
I stepped inside. I had begun to fill out the vandalism report when I
noticed a Bible on the end of her coffee table.

"So tell me, Ms. Beulah, do you read the Bible much?"

"Oh yes, Officer, I read it every day, morning and night."

"You know, Ms. Beulah, Jesus is coming back for us and coming back soon. I mean tonight we might not even finish making this report when"—I snapped my fingers—"just that quick, you and I will be heaven-bound. Just think, the boys responsible for terrifying you all this time might come back, break into your apartment, and find my clipboard and gun belt on the floor next to the brick they used, but they wouldn't find you and me because we'd be walking down those streets of gold. What do you think?"

Ms. Beulah wasn't much for talking at that point. You see, the more I talked about heaven and the rapture, the more I noticed something wonderful happening to her. Even as I spoke, her entire countenance began to change. A glow and warmth came over her that simply was amazing. She physically straightened up and jumped up and down while squealing like a four-year-old on Christmas morning! Tears began to stream down her worn, wrinkled face. But these were not tears of sorrow or fear but rather of profound joy, excitement, and hope for what her future held.

While we spoke, I looked around her apartment and noticed something else about Ms. Beulah. For one so full of joy and gratitude, she had absolutely nothing to show for it in the way of earthly treasures. The fact is that Ms. Beulah lived on welfare and did not even have a television. Her wardrobe consisted of three tattered, old housecoats and a few other articles of clothing that all appeared older than I was. Ms. Beulah's health was deteriorating. Her social life could best be described as lacking, for her husband had died several years earlier and she had no family and only a few friends in the area.

To make matters worse she was a frequent target of spiteful acts of vandalism carried out by groups of juveniles in the complex as demonstrated by the broken window to her apartment that night. And yet, in spite of it all, she still had that look in her eyes: a look of peace, contentment, and hope, a look that seemed to defy the very circumstances in which she lived.

I left Ms. Beulah that night knowing God had used a lonely old woman living on welfare to reveal to me His immeasurable love for His children—all His children. I stepped out of that tiny cockroach-infested apartment into the cold night air realizing that I had just been on holy ground. I would make it a point to visit Ms. Beulah often just to be in the presence of one who had truly found the secret of living a life of godliness with contentment.

In answer to prayer, Ms. Beulah was finally transferred out of that housing complex to a nursing home. It was at that nursing home that Ms. Beulah closed her eyes one last time on this side of eternity. When her eyes opened, she would find herself standing before her Savior and Lord Jesus Christ. The pain, the suffering, the loneliness, the fear, and the sleepless nights are not even memories for Ms. Beulah now, as she spends today, and every day, for all eternity walking down those streets of gold.

Ms. Beulah, I miss you and I thank you for the influence you have had on my life, the extent of which you will never know.

Little did I know that this was only one part of a two-part lesson God had in store for me.

Lesson 10: Godliness with contentment is truly great gain.

LESSON 11
EASY COME, EASY GO

Then He spoke a parable to them, saying: "The ground of a certain rich man yielded plentifully. And he thought within himself, saying, 'What shall I do, since I have no room to store my crops?' So he said, 'I will do this: I will pull down my barns and build greater, and there I will store all my crops and my goods. And I will say to my soul, "Soul, you have many goods laid up for many years; take your ease; eat, drink, and be merry."' But God said to him, 'Fool! This night your soul will be required of you; then whose will those things be which you have provided?' So is he who lays up treasure for himself, and is not rich toward God."

—Luke 12:16–21

"Get your hands up!" I shouted as beads of sweat began to stream down my face. My eyes locked on the lone figure sitting in the backseat of the Volvo my partner and I had just stopped after a five-minute pursuit.

"I said, get your hands up, now!" The figure in the backseat sat motionless. Slowly I made my way to the rear of the car with my gun pointed at its single occupant. We had managed to handcuff the three other men who had been in the car, but Tony, the fourth and final occupant, was not cooperating. My heart began to race as I walked up alongside the rear door.

"Get your hands up! I said, get your hands up! Do you hear me?" I commanded, but to no avail.

With my options all but gone, I had no other choice but to open Tony's door. As my heart raced, I reached for the door handle. I pulled on the handle and the door swung open. My gun was less than two feet from Tony's head as I scanned his body for weapons before lowering mine. Tony slowly turned his head in my direction.

"Man, what's wrong with you? Don't you realize I almost shot you?" It was while giving this guy a piece of my mind that I recognized that all-too-familiar thousand-yard stare.

"Can you hear me?" I asked.

Tony said nothing in response.

"Gary, I think we've got a problem here."

"What are you talking about?" Gary responded as he tried to keep watch on the three men we had pulled from the car.

Tony attempted to raise his hand to his chest but gave up after a couple of tries. I cautiously reached toward the expensive designer shirt Tony was wearing. By this time the thousand-yard stare seemed to give way to one of shock and fear that seemed to be growing nearer by the second.

I began to raise his shirt. Tony's breathing quickened as his chest began to move up and down in an exaggerated manner. I had lifted the shirt up to Tony's head by the time I saw the problem.

"Gary!" I shouted. "Get us a paramedic up here. This guy's been shot in the chest!" I watched helplessly as Tony knocked at death's door there in the backseat of the $25,000 sports car that I would find out later he had bought just days earlier. Tony would in fact die in that backseat at the age of seventeen.

Who was this young man who died such a tragic and premature death? It came as no great surprise when I discovered the shooting was drug related. Tony had apparently become a little too enterprising with his drug operation for his own good. In the process he broke one of the cardinal rules of drug dealing: "Do not overlap the competition."

Tony learned the hard way as he took a single shot to the chest during a drive-by shooting.

Before his death, Tony had done well selling drugs and as a result had received his share of the spoils: money, fine clothes, power, and women. He appeared to have it all. And to top it all off, he had his prized possession, the recently purchased Volvo that would become his deathbed.

Tony was the picture of success in the eyes of those around him, yet that success perished, as did his hope, as I stood over him, watching as he drifted out of this life and into eternity. Ironically, all the material possessions Tony had spent the better part of his very short life attempting to accumulate were slowly stripped away as his life came to its tragic end.

The fancy clothes were cut off by paramedics on the scene in a futile attempt to save Tony's life. The two thousand dollars in cash he had in his pocket was taken by homicide investigators and placed on a voucher, as were the fistful of gold necklaces and jewelry he was wearing. His brand new Volvo was towed by a city wrecker for investigation. And in the end, even his three friends abandoned him, heading for home with nothing more than one more story of how another "stick man" was gunned down.

Later that night I was reminded of that bumper sticker, "He who dies with the most toys, wins!" Tony had the "toys," but his eyes depicted anything but a winner. I then found myself thinking of Ms. Beulah, who died in utter poverty only to awaken to eternal wealth beyond measure in glory.

Lesson 11: How foolish it is to settle for the temporal "toys" of this world when Jesus has prepared eternal treasures in heaven for all who follow Him.

LESSON 12
ROAD TO DAMASCUS

Then Saul, still breathing threats and murder against the
disciples of the Lord, went to the high priest and asked
letters from him to the synagogues of Damascus, so that
if he found any who were of the Way, whether men or
women, he might bring them bound to Jerusalem. As he
journeyed he came near Damascus, and suddenly a light
shone around him from heaven.

—Acts 9:1–3

"One-four-two, respond to 1225 Tidewater Drive on a domestic
called in by an eight-year-old child."

"Ten-four, radio," I answered. "Send me some backup."

"One-three-two to radio, put me on the assist to one-four-two,"
my backup acknowledged.

The reason for the backup was not so much the call as it was for
the location. The apartment complex 1225 Tidewater Drive meant one
thing in the minds of police officers: Albert Jackson. And Albert Jackson
was synonymous with T-R-O-U-B-L-E.

Every neighborhood has one—a person who knows everything
about everybody and feels led to stick his or her nose where it doesn't
belong. Albert was that person for 1225 Tidewater Drive, only he wasn't
content with simply sticking his nose where it didn't belong. No, Albert
wasn't content until he stuck his feet and fists where they didn't belong

as well, which resulted in more than one trip to the emergency room for police officers and Albert alike.

Albert spoke a very violent game, and unfortunately he had the size, strength, and tenacity to back it up. For reasons known only to him, he had taken it upon himself to confront every police officer who crossed his path, and 1225 Tidewater Drive happened to fall right in the middle of Albert's path.

I remembered my last encounter with Albert. He began to run his mouth as he had done so many times before. Soon his words began to draw a crowd, which consistently triggered a predictable reaction from Albert, one of violence and rage. Albert quickly responded by pushing an officer. Within seconds, Albert was on the ground, having been subdued by half a dozen police officers. On this night, no one would be injured.

Several months had passed as I now pulled into 1225 Tidewater Drive. "Father, protect me," I quietly prayed while climbing out of my car. As I made my way to the apartment from which the eight-year-old had called, I scanned the shadows for Albert. I handled the call and began walking back to my police car. *Where is he?* I thought. I drove away that night thankful that God had protected me while at the same time curious about what had happened to Albert Jackson.

Two months later, my wife and I were invited to a fellow officer's home for a police officers' Bible study. As we stepped through the front door and into the warm, loving atmosphere of Christians coming together for a time of fun and fellowship, I noticed someone sitting in the corner of the room. Not believing my own eyes, I asked another officer who it was.

"You know him, Chris. That's Albert."

Something was wrong. This couldn't possibly be the same man I had wrestled with just a few months earlier. As the evening wore on, I began to see one of God's new creations. I stood baffled as I witnessed a love in Albert that was greater and unexplainably more consuming than the anger and rage to which I had grown accustomed had ever been. I found myself laughing with this man as we recalled "the good ol' days."

At the close of the evening we joined hands in prayer united in love and purpose. As we were praying, I remembered the question I had asked the Lord two months earlier: what happened to Albert? I now knew the answer. Jesus Christ had happened to Albert, and he would never be the same again.

Lesson 12: Be encouraged, that one who may seem beyond hope may yet be on the road to Damascus.

LESSON 13
THREE TICKETS AND A LITTLE HOPE

Therefore, if anyone is in Christ, he is a new creation; old things have passed away; behold, all things have become new.

—2 Corinthians 5:17

It had been a hectic, fast-paced shift and I was exhausted, both physically and mentally. I had been looking forward to going home when Murphy's Law struck yet again. While heading in to the station, minding my own business, a beat-up, old, brown two-door sedan sailed past me as if it were attempting to take flight. *I don't believe this,* I thought, as I activated my lights and siren and sped up to catch the speeding violator.

"Good evening, sir. Can I see your license and the registration to your car?" I asked, trying to hide the disgust in my voice at having stopped this man so close to relief time.

"Yeah—I mean, yes, sir, I know it's here someplace."

As the man fumbled through his wallet and then the glove box to the old sedan, I began to detect the odor of alcohol coming from inside the car. *Oh well, Chris—so much for going home on time,* I thought.

"What is your name?" I asked.

"Willie Johnson, sir," he replied.

"I kind of get the feeling, Mr. Johnson, that you don't have a license, or if you do, it's suspended, right?"

Mr. Johnson dropped his head before admitting that his license was suspended. "Have you had any alcohol to drink tonight, Mr. Johnson?"

"Yes, sir, I had a couple beers, but that was over two hours ago, sir."

I asked Mr. Johnson to step out of his car and then spent the next few minutes conducting a field sobriety test to see if the alcohol he had consumed earlier had impaired his ability to drive. After the lengthy test, I told him to have a seat in the back of my police car.

"So tell me, Willie, are you an alcoholic?"

"Yeah, I am, sir. If I could walk away from it, I would, but I can't. No matter how hard I try, I just can't." Willie's voice was filled with a real sense of despair.

I suddenly realized that it was no mere coincidence that Willie Johnson had sped by me that evening. Sensing God had opened a door I went for broke. "Willie, have you tried turning to God for help?"

"Nothing against you, Officer uh ..."

"Amos, Chris Amos," I interrupted.

"Officer Amos, I'm from a family of religious people, and they have come down on me hard about my drinking and all. I've tried to ask God for help, but ..." Tears began to form in the bloodshot eyes of this forty-year-old man. "But He just don't care, I guess."

I began to spell out to Willie God's plan of salvation and how it was important for him not only to confess and repent for his life of sin, but to really understand and have the faith to believe that Jesus cared so much that He died for him, Willie Johnson, the alcoholic. He needed to believe that the blood of Jesus could cleanse him of all the filth that beer, wine, and liquor had been drowning him in all these years.

"That's it! That's it! That's it!" Willie began shouting as his face lit up like a Fourth of July fireworks show.

"Willie!" I shouted back. "What's it?"

"For years people have told me that I was a sinner and booze was of the devil, but nobody ever showed me what I was supposed to do about it!"

You see, Willie knew John 3:16, and he knew all about the Crucifixion and Resurrection of Jesus, but somehow in the midst of all that knowledge, he missed the most important part of the story. Jesus died for Willie Johnson, the alcoholic. Jesus rose for Willie Johnson, the alcoholic. And Jesus now wanted to live in Willie Johnson and set him free from the stronghold of alcohol.

I looked into the tear-filled eyes of this middle-aged man and said, "Willie, I want to lead you in a sinner's prayer, but you have got to make the choice. Jesus died and rose for you, but that means nothing unless you invite Him into your heart. Do you understand?"

"Yes," Willie answered before closing his eyes and bowing his head.

For the next few minutes the backseat of that police car became an altar of prayer as Willie invited Jesus Christ into his heart as his personal Savior and Lord.

I would see Willie a month later in court.

"Officer Amos, I'm not exactly sure about all that's happened to me since you wrote me those tickets, but something big is goin' on inside me," Willie exclaimed with a grin from ear to ear and a glow in his eyes that sent goose bumps down my back.

"Well, Willie, if you have a few minutes, I'll tell you what's going on," and with that we walked out of the courtroom and into the noonday radiance of a beautiful summer afternoon.

Lesson 13: It is often during the inconveniences of life that God desires to be most active in the lives of His children.

LESSON 14
EXPECT IT WHEN YOU LEAST EXPECT IT

Be sober, be vigilant; because your adversary the devil walks about like a roaring lion, seeking whom he may devour.

—1 Peter 5:8

My knocks at the door went unanswered by the elderly woman inside. We could hear her rustling around inside her second-floor apartment, but we could not get her to answer the door. I knocked once more, hoping she would cooperate and open it.

"Ms. Brown, please open the door. It's the police. We're here to help you," I assured her, but to no avail.

"It doesn't look like she's going to be very helpful," another officer on the scene piped up.

"Well, whether she cooperates or not, she's coming with us," Robin, a mental health evaluator, responded.

"Hey, she can't be all that crazy," I mused. "She's smart enough not to open the door."

"Officer Amos, do you think you could climb onto her balcony and try to get in that way?" Robin asked.

"It wouldn't hurt to try," I answered.

A few minutes later I was on Ms. Brown's balcony quietly opening her sliding-glass door. Once inside her apartment I made a beeline for the front door. After unlocking the door and letting the others in, the three of us began to call Ms. Brown by name as we cautiously made our way down a hall toward her back bedroom.

"Ms. Brown," Robin called, "you are going to have to come with us to the hospital to speak with some doctors, okay?"

Ms. Brown came walking out of her bedroom, not the least bit impressed with our reason for being there. "What are you doing in my house?"

"Well, Ms. Brown, we are here to pick you up and take you to the hospital," I answered as pleasantly as possible.

"Child!" Ms. Brown said. "You ain't picking me up nowhere! I've got two good legs of my own to stand on."

Oops, poor choice of words, I thought.

The three of us spent the next several minutes trying to coax Ms. Brown into coming with us. She didn't buy it. After all, she said, she didn't even have a new pair of shoes to wear for the occasion. I went back into her bedroom closet and saw a stack of shoes four feet tall, still in the boxes. The lightbulb suddenly clicked on.

Ms. Brown had made it to the front room in her apartment but no farther, and she sat on her sofa determined not to budge. That is, until she saw my smiling face walking toward her, carrying a shoe box. Her eyes began to sparkle with excitement as I handed her the black-and-gray box.

"For me?" Ms. Brown asked.

"Yes, ma'am," I answered.

"Oh, child, you shouldn't have," Ms. Brown responded, giddy as a schoolgirl.

Leaving well enough alone I told Ms. Brown she was quite welcome before helping her put on her "new" shoes. Once finished, Ms. Brown picked up her purse and walked out her front door. She made it halfway down the hall leading to the stairwell before she had a change of heart.

"New shoes or not, I'm not going!" Without warning she fell to the ground like a sack of potatoes. *It's time for plan B,* I thought as I scooped Ms. Brown up in my arms and headed down the stairs.

Halfway down Ms. Brown began hitting me in the head with her right hand. This would not have been so painful had it not been for one little detail … She had broken her wrist a few weeks earlier, and her right hand was in a very hard cast. I did all I could to protect myself from her ongoing barrage of punches, just short of dropping her down a flight of stairs. After about five real good, solid blows, and I mean *solid,* to the top of my head, she stopped. Hey, even Muhammad Ali had to catch his breath. I let out a sigh of relief, thinking the worst was over. I was wrong.

We finally reached the base of the stairs, where I stopped to catch my breath. Without warning Ms. Brown snapped her head around in the direction of my face and began to lunge repeatedly toward my nose, her mouth opening and closing like a snapping turtle. The mere sight of this precious little ol' seventy-five-year-old grandmother lunging back and forth like a hissing cobra snake as she tried desperately to bite a chunk out of my nose gave fear a whole new meaning. Fortunately, she had removed her dentures earlier that evening, so this threat was not quite as serious as it could have been. *For some reason this particular scenario was never covered in the police academy,* I thought while struggling to withstand the physical onslaught from this seemingly harmless old woman. Aunt Bee, she was not.

The other officer on the scene pulled her police car up onto the grass in front of the apartment building. She then opened the door to the building, and out Ms. Brown and I went as she continued snapping at me. I managed to set Ms. Brown in the back of the police car, her feet hanging out the side.

"Ms. Brown, will you please swing your feet into the car so I can close the door?" I asked.

I dropped my head for a split second just to relax the throbbing muscles in my neck. Mistake. No sooner had I looked down than Ms. Brown pulled both of her legs up to her chest. Rather than swinging them around and into the car, she kicked them up and out of the car as hard as she could. Now my head was the one doing the snapping as she caught me square on the jaw with both feet. Once I remembered who I was, where I was, and why I was there, I pushed her legs back into the car and slammed the door shut.

I followed the car carrying Ms. Brown to the hospital. In the event she needed someone to hit, bite, or kick, I wanted to be there for her. Robin met us at the hospital. She had gone on ahead just to make sure there were sufficient orderlies to handle Ms. Brown. We pulled up, and to my surprise, Ms. Brown quietly climbed out of the police car, prim and proper, before sitting in the wheelchair provided. I wished her my best before turning to walk away.

Smack! I felt something hit the back of my head. As I turned to see what had happened, *smack!* I felt it again. Before I could say a word, Ms. Brown angrily shouted, "Child, you can keep the shoes! I've got a pair just like them at home!"

I handed the shoes to an orderly before quickly slipping into my police car, where I spent the better part of the night licking my wounds.

Lesson 14: Sin may not always bark, but trust me ... it always, always, always bites!

LESSON 15
DIFFERENT MASK, SAME FACE

And no wonder! For Satan himself transforms himself into an angel of light. Therefore it is no great thing if his ministers also transform themselves into ministers of righteousness, whose end will be according to their works.

—2 Corinthians 11:14–15

"I'd shoot every one of you if I had a gun!" a woman yelled.

"You better not come back out here tonight if you know what's good for you," another warned.

"We got to fight back, we got to fight five-oh," a third began to scream.

The anger felt by those within this mob quickly turned to unbridled rage as the rumor spread that police officers had beaten a juvenile arrested for stealing a car.

"Kill a cop! Kill a cop!" the crowd began to chant.

Outnumbered and fearing that we were about to lose control of an already bad situation, my partner picked up his radio. "Dispatcher, get us help, now!" The radio came alive as officer after officer answered the urgent plea for help.

Within minutes police cars were converging on our location from every direction. The show of force did nothing but incite the crowd even more as it swelled to more than 150 people.

"Take off that gun and badge and then let's see how tough you are," a teenager shouted to me.

"Mike," I said to the officer next to me, "it wouldn't hurt my feelings if the rapture came right now and I could leave a lot more behind than just this gun and badge." as I tried to bring a little humor to a tense situation.

"You and me both, Chris, but don't count on it, partner." Mike answered.

The barrage of threats hurled our way eventually faded as residents grew tired and went back inside their apartments. Unfortunately, the toll of those threats on the officers present did not end as easily.

The anger, hatred, and rage directed toward those of us who were just trying to do our jobs was more than a little disheartening. I left that neighborhood feeling as though I had been put through the ringer.

One week later I found myself facing another group of people, only these were not folks enraged at the police. On the contrary, this group was much smaller and more united in purpose. This group was protesting the opening of an abortion clinic in town. Many of the officers detailed to this pro-life demonstration had been at the mini-riot the week before. I reminded the officers of the discretion we had exercised at the riot and encouraged them to do likewise at this demonstration.

The demonstration was moving along in an orderly and peaceful manner when without warning two of the demonstrators turned their attention toward myself and another officer.

"Norfolk's finest," a middle-aged man shouted as he stared directly at me. "You should be arresting drug dealers and child molesters, and look at you, protecting baby killers." And then with a coldness and callousness that caught me off guard, the man warned, "God is going to judge you for this." A second demonstrator took out a camera and began to take our pictures as she too warned us of the price we would pay for protecting "baby killers."

My mind raced back to the week before. A different setting, a different purpose, a different group of people, and yet the same anger, the same hatred, and the same rage had been demonstrated. The earlier situation sprang from a lie, the second from the truth, and yet the threats directed toward me both times were in a sense very, very similar.

I tried to see Jesus in the words and actions of this man and woman, but my search was in vain. *Such an important cause,* I thought, *but fueled by such hatred.* Satan must have been pleased not only with what was happening within the clinic that day, but also with what was happening without.

Lesson 15: Hatred may wear many different masks, but behind each one is the same face, that of Satan himself.

LESSON 16
THE HILL

Concerning this thing I pleaded with the Lord three times that it might depart from me. And He said to me, "My grace is sufficient for you, for My strength is made perfect in weakness." Therefore most gladly I will rather boast in my infirmities, that the power of Christ may rest upon me. Therefore I take pleasure in infirmities, in reproaches, in needs, in persecutions, in distresses, for Christ's sake. For when I am weak, then I am strong.

—2 Corinthians 12:8–10

It was unassuming enough, a weed-strewn hill that in its prime was the site on which the old city incinerator stood. Those days have long since passed, and now what once was filled with the hustle and bustle of city employees busy at work burning debris lies vacant as it overlooks the mouth of the Elizabeth River. The main road leading to the top was removed years ago, and the dirt road that remains is no longer in use. To reach the top one must ride a bike or walk. Once at the top there is cut into its side a narrow dirt path, filled with ruts and other obstacles, that drops 200 feet to the Elizabeth River below. It was on this 200-foot dirt path that God taught me a remarkable lesson.

You see, several officers of the mountain bike unit had taken on the ascension of this dirt path as the ultimate challenge. Unfortunately, all takers had failed to conquer this intimidating challenge. Being the experienced bike cop that I am, I took one look at the hill before shrugging it off as "a piece of cake, no problem—gravy, gentlemen, gravy." With that, I carefully crept down the dirt path in an attempt to avoid injury. Once firmly footed at the bottom of the hill, I turned, looking back up to the top.

Hmm, I said to myself. *It does appear, Chris, that it is quite a bit longer from the bottom looking up than from the top looking down. But, hey, no problem. Remember, piece of cake, right? Gravy, Chris, gravy.*

I strapped my feet in, shifted down to an easier gear, and began the ascent of the hill. Halfway up it dawned on me. This wasn't just any ordinary hill. No, on the contrary, this was the Pikes Peak of the East Coast. Well, at least that's what my body was telling me as my legs burned and my heart seemed to be trying to beat right out of my chest.

Fifty feet from the top my legs, mind, and bike all came to a mutual agreement: we quit! This is not a good thing when on the side of a steep, rut-filled, dirt path 150 feet above sea level. I managed to abandon ship, or in my case bike, before both bike and rider found themselves hurtling down the hill at a high speed, backward. I conceded defeat this day but vowed to return.

Unfortunately, for me, I did return—not just once, but several more times and with the same results, when suddenly it happened. I had well over a dozen failed attempts under my belt when I hit the hill yet again. This attempt would be different from any other, because this time I was already exhausted. I had nothing to give in the way of energy or strength, and yet for some reason I continued my cautious descent to the bottom of the hill.

As I waited to begin yet another attempt at reaching the summit (I use the term *summit* because as far as I was concerned, the hill had become a full-blown mountain) I said a simple prayer: "God, my tank is empty. If I make it up this thing, it will be because of you—period!"

I turned my bike toward the path and began to pedal. My legs immediately began to burn as sweat rolled down my face. *Keep pedaling Chris, keep pedaling.* Halfway up the hill it was as if I could feel hands pressing down on my legs. I began to pick up speed during the steepest part of the climb. The burning suddenly stopped, as did my usual gasping for air. For lack of better words, I felt as though I was literally being propelled up the side of the hill. The officer with me that day stood at the top looking down in utter amazement as I made my way toward him effortlessly. I reached the top that day, and yet I realized "I" didn't do it.

"How did you do it, Chris?" Immanuel asked.

"Well, Immanuel, this may sound kind of strange, but I didn't."

"What do you mean, you didn't? You did do it, and you weren't even straining. You looked like you could have kept on going up another hill."

"Well, I think I know what Paul was talking about in the Bible when he said, 'For when I am weak then I am strong.' I mean, God waited until I was totally exhausted as far as my own willpower, energy, and effort went before He worked His perfect power in my weakness. Immanuel, you've seen me fail a dozen times trying to climb this hill, and the one time I succeeded, I can't even take credit for it. I mean, I was just too tired to do what just happened."

"What are you talking about?" Immanuel asked, now totally confused.

"Well, Immanuel, it's like this ..." and so God opened yet another door as I shared with Immanuel the Good News of Jesus Christ.

As we turned and rode away from the hill, the words of Jesus echoed in my mind: "My grace is sufficient for thee, for my strength is made perfect in weakness."

Lesson 16: The secret to true strength is total dependence on the Lord, in every area of life.

LESSON 17
"I HAD HIM!"

"Blessed *is* the man who trusts in the LORD, and whose hope is the LORD."

—Jeremiah 17:7

"Open the door, Wilbert," I encouraged while standing by the back door of this man's apartment. Wilbert, like most folks, took the "I'll hide and they'll go away" approach, and so I was left with no other choice than to continue pleading.

"Wilbert, will you please open the door? I'm not going to hurt you. I'm here to help."

Suddenly the back door opened and standing before me was Wilbert Williams. I was a little taken aback at first. I mean, I didn't really expect him to actually do it.

Wilbert was a tall, muscular man in his thirties who appeared more than capable of snapping me in two if he so desired. About six feet three inches tall and 230 pounds, Wilbert was an imposing figure by any standard. He seemed better suited to playing linebacker in the NFL than to be standing in front of me without so much as a stitch of clothes on. Realizing this, I did what any sane person would do: I called for help.

You see, Wilbert had been engaged in some pretty erratic behavior earlier in the day that resulted in my being dispatched to his apartment to serve a temporary detention order. Apparently, Wilbert had only a few of hours earlier decided to run a few laps around his apartment building, in his birthday suit. As I watched Wilbert step into the doorway, I could tell he hadn't bothered to change for me.

I took a step toward the open door. *Slam!* Oh well—so much for this ending early. I moved to the kitchen window, hoping I could see what Wilbert was up to. It did appear as if he had experienced a slight mood swing from "I'll hide and they'll go away" to "Come and get me!"

"One-four-three to radio," I called, a tone of urgency in my voice.

"Go ahead, one-four-three," the dispatcher responded.

"Could you send me some backup and a supervisor? My detainee does not want to be detained."

I moved to Wilbert's kitchen window to see what he was up to. While standing there, I heard the sound of glass breaking. I moved closer, hoping to get a better look. Mistake! As I leaned toward the window, a chair suddenly appeared, flying through the air at a very high rate of speed, right at me. I ducked as the chair crashed against a wall, just missing the window by inches.

"One-four-three to the units responding to my location, can you step it up? This guy is getting violent."

"Wilbert, relax," I called. "You worked hard for that furniture. You don't want to ..." My words of comfort were interrupted as a second chair came flying in my direction. *Crash!* The chair fell to the floor after hitting the wall. When all else fails, use reverse psychology, right? Wrong! I made the mistake of pointing out a third chair that Wilbert had not yet thrown. Unfortunately, he was more than happy to send this third chair flying across the room in my direction as I quickly found myself hitting the dirt once again. Within minutes, Wilbert had thrown the three chairs back into the hallway and begun working on a huge kitchen cupboard that had to weigh every bit of two hundred pounds.

"Wilbert, seriously now, I don't think you want to do ..." *Kaboom!* Too late—he did. The cupboard hit the hard tiled floor like a falling meteor, sending broken pieces of glass, chipped plates, and several small cans of food everywhere. Fortunately, the cans of food apparently were too small to be bothered with by this man intent on throwing everything in sight.

"One-four-two to one-four-three, do we have a key yet to this guy's apartment?" I radioed to the officer who was now on the scene standing by the front door.

"Not yet. The supervisor is having the rental manager bring one to our location."

"Okay, the sooner the better."

Once the kitchen was ransacked, Wilbert climbed into the kitchen sink, curled up in a ball, and began to wash himself. To wash an infant in the kitchen sink is one thing. To watch as a man big enough to play linebacker in the NFL attempted to do likewise is quite another. I watched as Wilbert filled a flowerpot with water. Wilbert then dipped his hand into the muddy mess and began smearing the mixture of water and potting soil from head to toe. Fortunately, by this time, additional help had arrived and my backup unit and I were joined by four additional officers.

I began to brief the two officers who had come around back to help me. While talking with them, a gentleman walked up. "Excuse me, Officer, can I help?" he asked.

"Who are you?" one of the officers responded.

"My name is Jerry Williams; I'm Wilbert's younger brother." Jerry filled us in on his older brother's mental history. As he spoke, I couldn't help but think of the demon-possessed man Jesus set free at the expense of a large herd of pigs.

"If you give me a chance," Jerry suggested, "I know I can talk him into coming outside. I guarantee it."

"Sounds good to me, but be careful—we don't know what he's going to do next," the officer answered.

Jerry walked over to the window. "Wilbert, what's gotten into you? Get out of that sink, put some clothes on, and open the door. Do you understand?"

Apparently Wilbert didn't respond quickly enough to his brother's commands, because without warning Jerry lunged through the window and wrapped both hands around Wilbert's waist in an attempt to pull this mountain of a man out the kitchen window. Just as quickly, Wilbert responded by picking up the nearest thing possible—a toaster—and began beating Jerry in the head with it. I found myself engaged in a pretty intense tug-of-war as we three officers struggled to pull Jerry out the window. With one final heave Jerry broke his grip on Wilbert and was pulled to safety.

"Why did you do that?" Jerry snapped as if angered by our actions. "I had him!"

"Yeah, I'll say you had him all right. If you had had him any longer, you would be in a coma," an officer snapped back as we watched in disbelief as this battered, beaten, and bruised man attempted to catch his breath.

Wilbert eventually tried to make a run for it out the front door and into the waiting arms of three police officers, two paramedics, and one mental health evaluator. He was taken to the hospital for evaluation. From there he was sent to the state mental hospital, again.

Maybe, just maybe, Wilbert met Jesus there. I hope that's not wishful thinking, but then again the demon-possessed man probably didn't have a meeting with the Son of God planned in his appointment book, either.

Lesson 17: Satan has a word for those who are confident in their own abilities to defeat him: *victim!*

LESSON 18
OPEN YOUR EYES

But even if our gospel is veiled, it is veiled to those who are perishing, whose minds the god of this age has blinded, who do not believe, lest the light of the gospel of the glory of Christ, who is the image of God, should shine on them.

—2 Corinthians 4:3–4

Her name was Sandy. She was one of the regulars at the city jail. Her crime of choice: being drunk in public. I can count on one hand the number of times I saw Sandy sober. It would take both hands and feet to count the number of times I had seen her in a drunken stupor. There had been many opportunities for Sandy to receive help through counseling, but she refused every time.

On this night my partner and I responded to the almost weekly call to Sandy's apartment to referee an argument between her and her alcoholic boyfriend, Robert. Oh, I had tried during those rare moments of sobriety to share with Sandy the Good News of Jesus Christ, but they always seemed few and far between, at best.

As my partner and I stood at the door, we could hear Sandy and Robert's usual barrage of threats and accusations. Both were obviously intoxicated.

"Sandy, open the door. It's the police," my partner said while knocking.

The door flew open and there stood Sandy: thirty-five years old, but with a face that seemed almost twice that. Her breath burned with the odor of alcohol as her eyes, glassy and bloodshot, struggled to focus on the two men standing in front of her. She appeared to be wearing the same T-shirt and blue jeans that I had seen her in a few days earlier, and from the smell of them, I doubt she had changed since.

After realizing who we were, Sandy turned and staggered to her bed, as was her normal response upon the arrival of the police. My partner and I followed her down the hall and into her bedroom as we had countless times before. I tried to encourage Sandy as best I could and remind her that Jesus wanted her just as she was before she interrupted.

"Jesus doesn't love me. Nobody loves me," she said as tears ran down her face. "I've asked God to show me, to prove to me He loves me, but He can't or He won't." She was sobbing now.

"Sandy, Jesus died for you! That's proof enough," I answered, hoping in some small way that would register with her.

After determining she and Robert would make it through the night, we turned to leave. Suddenly, Sandy began to beg us to stay.

"Please don't leave me, please don't leave me, please stay! I'm so afraid I'm going to die. Please don't leave me," and so she continued to plead as my partner and I left that night. Her desperate pleas for help echoed in my mind in the weeks to come—pleas of a woman who wanted to wake up from a never-ending alcoholic nightmare, and yet was unable or unwilling to do so.

Two weeks later, Sandy was arrested again for being drunk in public. While sleeping in a holding cell in the city jail, she choked to death on her own vomit. She died as she had lived: alone, drunk, and seemingly without hope. She lived her life searching for and yet never seeing the hope found in Jesus Christ.

I, like Sandy, had also turned to God asking and in fact begging for a sign to assure me that He wanted to help, that He cared about me, that He actually loved me. I spent hours on my knees weeping as I pleaded with God to show me a sign of His love. I can clearly remember feeling emptier and more depressed after having finished those prayers than I had felt before I began. I too was seeking a sign from God confirming His love for me. A streak of lightning, rolling thunder, or a magnificent rainbow—I would have accepted anything. I know now something that, like Sandy, I did not know then: "For God so loved the world that He gave His one and only Son that whosoever believes in Him shall not perish, but have everlasting life." God gave me something of far greater value than any natural phenomenon. He gave His Son, Jesus Christ.

I spent years seeking proof of God's love for me when in fact God had already demonstrated His love for me and all of mankind by allowing His one and only Son, Jesus Christ, to be tortured and executed on an old rugged cross nearly two thousand years ago. God does not need to prove to any man, woman, or child His love for them. That has already been done. It is time for us to flesh out our love for Him.

To those individuals who are hurting and are desperately searching for proof that God cares about the pain, loneliness, and suffering they are experiencing, God not only cares but cares so much that He allowed His perfect, sinless, spotless Son to experience far more pain, loneliness, and suffering than we ever could.

Lesson 18: The only thing more frustrating than searching for something that is not there is failing to see something that is. Open your eyes. Jesus is there.

LESSON 19

WHEN EYES SPEAK LOUDER
THAN WORDS

... that the God of our Lord Jesus Christ, the Father of glory, may give to you the spirit of wisdom and revelation in the knowledge of Him, the eyes of your understanding being enlightened; that you may know what is the hope of His calling, what are the riches of the glory of His inheritance in the saints, and what is the exceeding greatness of His power toward us who believe, according to the working of His mighty power.

—Ephesians 1:17–19

So much is said through the eyes of a man. It is the eyes that speak truth when the mind and mouth are intent on doing otherwise. And, it is in the eyes of men addicted that I am most reminded of my own past. Oh, they speak of being fine and doing well, but their eyes tell another story, one of pain, despair, and hopelessness.

"I'm okay, Officer. I haven't smoked cracked for three months. I gave it up, you know. I'm not into that anymore."

"Officer, I'm straight. I've got five years hanging over my head, and I'm not using heroin no more."

"I quit drinking after the last time you arrested me. I'm not going to jail again."

And so their empty promises and assurances go when all the while their eyes are saying, "Is there any hope? Please answer me. Is there any hope?"

As I speak of Jesus and the hope found in Him, many quickly brush Him off as impractical, irrelevant, or too distant and uncaring to really matter. Others literally begin to weep. Yet even among these, very few really believe that Jesus is willing to and capable of making a difference in their life.

As I look into the eyes of these desperate men, I remember all too clearly how I, too, suffered from a life-destroying addiction. Mine began at the age of ten and came to a near tragic end at the age of twenty-four as I came within a fraction of an inch of committing suicide. My addiction was to pornography, and yet it was as consuming and overpowering as any addiction to alcohol, cocaine, or heroin could possibly be. I, too, spoke the words others wanted to hear when in reality, my eyes told of a man slowly dying within.

The names and faces are far too many to count, but that look, that despair-ridden look of death from within, appeared on each one. There was the occasional victory, the occasional captive set free by the grace of God, but that was the exception. Most seemed unwilling to believe that true victory and freedom were really possible.

I also felt hopeless and destined for hell when suddenly and without warning God removed the spiritual blinders that Satan had used to keep me in darkness and despair. Once they were removed, I saw myself as a sinner standing in the shadow of a cross. And there at its base, I saw something far more personal than the anonymous sins of the world. I found myself staring at the secret life of sin that I had led. The lies, the deception, the filth—it was all there. It was then that I realized Jesus had done more than die for the nameless, faceless men and women, young and old, of this world. He died for the sins of Chris Amos.

As I look into their eyes now, I am reminded of my own past—the pain and despair, the suffering and hopelessness, the frustration and embarrassment—and then just as quickly, I am reminded of that old rugged cross on which my sins were nailed, and their sins, too.

Lesson 19: There are two things about a person the eyes cannot hide, the presence of hope and the presence of hopelessness.

LESSON 20
WHEN IT HURTS TO REMEMBER

"For I will be merciful to their unrighteousness, and their sins and their lawless deeds I will remember no more."

—Hebrews 8:12

"**H**ey! Stop that car," Vic yelled as the car zoomed past.

In a car, that would have been no problem, but on a bike ... it's a different story. Vic had seen the car stopped in an area known as Weed Alley, so named because of the large amount of marijuana sold and bought there. The occupants of the car had been approached by a known marijuana dealer. After seeing Vic, the car quickly sped away, passing my partner and me.

My partner quickly radioed for help as the car began to pull away. "Any unit around Virginia Beach and Park? We are trying to stop a white two-door sedan being driven by a white male."

"One-two-three, I'm coming up to that location now. Dispatcher, put me on an assist to that unit." The flashing lights and wailing siren of the police car was a great relief, as my partner and I were quickly losing steam while attempting to keep the car in sight.

Within minutes, the car was pulled over by two marked police cars. A few minutes after the stop, my partner and I arrived at the scene, after sprinting nearly two miles on our bikes.

The two occupants were asked to step out of the car. I began to talk to the female passenger. "So what's your name?"

"My name is Mary, sir. Mary O'Neil."

"Where are you coming from, Mary?"

"I'm not sure. We got a little lost and ended up on some back streets."

The back streets she was referring to just happened to be Weed Alley.

"Okay, now tell me the truth. I know you were on that back street for the sole purpose of buying marijuana, right?"

No response.

"Good—at least we agree on something. The question I have is, Did you have time to actually buy the pot or not?"

"Sir, that is why we were there, but to tell you the truth—"

"Please do," I interrupted.

"Yes, sir, as I was saying, Officer Amos, we didn't have a chance to buy any, because you showed up."

As I began to talk with this forty-five-year-old woman, I began to learn of a person who had led a hard life, and the look of pain and despair in her eyes quietly attested to the words that she spoke.

"I had a couple of kids, but I lost them both early."

"Did they die at birth?" I asked.

"No. I was forced to give my son up to the social services when he was two because I was going through a nervous breakdown and wasn't fit to be a parent." The words she spoke were laced with pain, humiliation, and guilt. "My second child was a baby girl, but I had to give her up for adoption at birth."

God, if ever there were a person who needed your unconditional love, Mary is that person, I prayed silently as Mary continued.

"My son is twenty-five now and my daughter is twenty-one, but I don't know where they are. I haven't seen them since I lost them. I pray one day that I can see them again, just to tell them I'm sorry and that I love them."

That's it, Lord. She's speaking your language now.

"Mary, do you know there is someone who loves you just as you are? There is someone who loves you with all your faults, failures, and mistakes. There is someone who is willing and eager to forgive you of every sin you have ever committed. There is someone who can take the filth and stench of your past and wash it white as snow." As I quietly spoke these words of hope, Mary dropped her head and began to weep. "Mary, do you know who I am talking about?"

"Yes, sir," she whimpered. "God."

As I continued to share with Mary, it was as if a golden ray of hope began to pierce the darkness and despair hidden in her eyes. Oh, the weeping continued, but the tears were not simply tears of regret, shame, and despair. No, the tears were also of one daring to believe there really was hope, having heard, perhaps for the very first time, of a Savior who loved her enough to die on a cross so that she might be set free from a life of sin, bad decisions, and tragic mistakes, and experience the unconditional love of almighty God.

As I watched this woman broken by conviction, it was as if I could sense Jesus Christ Himself standing with His arm around her, saying, "Where are your accusers now, Mary? Oh, Mary, they are gone. Now go, my child, and sin no more."

Lesson 20: God desires that we remember our past. Satan wants us to drive down our tent stakes and live there.

LESSON 21
UNFORGIVING

Then Peter came to Him and said, "Lord, how often shall my brother sin against me, and I forgive him? Up to seven times?" Jesus said to him, "I do not say to you, up to seven times, but up to seventy times seven."

—Matthew 18:21–22

The small wooden plaque propped up on the end table caught my attention. It simply read, "Don't bother me—I'm having a crisis." The message was almost prophetic for the family in whose house it stood. The middle-aged couple had been having problems. I guess you could even call it a crisis. The tension between the two had risen greatly during the previous days. On this day, their crisis had become such that the police responded to their home to referee a very loud, profanity-laced argument. The officers who responded left the home after both Becky and Alex asked them to do so. I arrived at the home several hours later on what turned out to be the most devastating crisis of this couple's marriage.

Becky, her eyes bloodshot and watered with tears, attempted with great difficulty to explain to us what had happened.

"We had been fighting earlier today, and I told him to go sleep in the doghouse. I stormed out of the room and went into our back bedroom to take a nap." Becky continued, "When I got up a couple

73

hours later, I couldn't find him. I thought maybe he went down to the beach and was fishing with his buddies or maybe he went to one of the bars. I waited a while, and then I went out looking for him. He wasn't on the beach or at any of the bars, so I came home."

Becky's face tightened as she began to share what happened next.

"When I got home, I checked the house again, but couldn't find him. I thought that maybe he was in the backyard by the pool, so I got a candle and went out back. I saw him"—her voice began to crack—"sleeping in the doghouse. I went over there to tell him to come inside. I called him, but he didn't answer. I bent down and looked in the doghouse …"

By now, Becky's whole body was shaking as her words turned into a cry of pain and anguish. Alex had crawled into the doghouse shortly after their earlier argument. No one knows how long he was there thinking about the anger, frustration, bitterness, and resentment that had become the norm for their marriage. Alex, unforgiving and unforgiven, put a twelve-gauge shotgun to his head and pulled the trigger. Becky, unforgiving and unforgiven, had discovered her husband's lifeless body.

As I left that night, I watched as Becky's brother pulled up in front of the house. He met Becky in the middle of the front yard. "What happened?" I heard him ask.

"He shot himself. He's dead. That no good … is dead," Becky replied, her voice full of a mixture of anger and rage, shock, disbelief, and pain before she passed out in her brother's arms.

How many lives must be destroyed, marriages divided, and families shattered before we realize we *must* forgive others as Christ forgave us? Would Alex be alive today had he and Becky not allowed the sun to set on their anger? What do you think?

Lesson 21: Nearly two thousand years ago, Jesus asked His Father to forgive those who had turned against Him. Two thousand years later, He asks us to do likewise. His Father listened. Will we?

LESSON 22

THE GOD OF SECOND CHANCES

Now the word of the LORD came to Jonah the second
time, saying, ...

—Jonah 3:1

"Hey, have you seen my watch?" the man asked.
I thought the question was a bit strange, considering the
fact that I patrol an area that covers several city blocks and includes
thirty thousand people. What made even less sense was that the question
came from a complete stranger.

"No, sorry, man, I sure haven't. What does it look like?"

"Well, ahhh, it doesn't have any special markings. Never mind."

It didn't take long before I realized that this guy was missing more
than just his watch.

"So, what's your name?" I asked.

"Vernon Hobbs, sir."

"Vernon, do you live around here?"

"I'm staying at the Union Mission while I try to get my job
back."

The more we talked, the more I learned about Vernon Hobbs.
Vernon at one time had a pretty good job until he was admitted to a
psychiatric hospital for evaluation. Apparently, Vernon had decided
one day while at work to take his clothes off and set them on fire. This

did not go over well with his employer. Within a few minutes after having done so, Vernon found himself not only detained for a mental evaluation by the police but also without a job.

When Vernon had finished speaking, he said good-bye before quietly turning and continuing on his way down the street. I had a sick feeling in the pit of my stomach as I watched Vernon turn a corner and disappear. I had what he was really looking for, and it was not a lost watch, but I had blown the opportunity to share it.

I quickly forgot about Vernon amid the hustle and bustle of the day—that is, until I heard over the radio another police officer requesting help with a violent suspect. By the description given we quickly realized the suspect in question was Vernon Hobbs. Apparently, after speaking with Dave and me, Vernon had continued down the street for about a mile until he came to a convenience store. Vernon then walked up to the Dumpster next to the store and attempted repeatedly to set it on fire.

Shortly thereafter, Vernon found himself in the backseat of a police car awaiting a mental evaluation, and I found myself angry that I had not taken the time to share my message of hope with Vernon when given the chance. I couldn't help but think that if only I had shared, Vernon would not have been in the position he was in. I quietly asked God to forgive me for what I had failed to do and, if possible, to give me one more opportunity to speak with Vernon. With that, I headed in to the station for relief.

As I pulled into the parking lot of the police station, it was as if God said, "Chris, you blew it the first time, but I love you enough and I love Vernon enough to give you both a second chance. What are you going to do about it?" I approached the station door, and to my disbelief, there sat Vernon Hobbs, secured both with handcuffs and leg shackles in the backseat of a police car. I had time for a real quick prayer before approaching Vernon.

"Vernon, what in the world have you done?"

Vernon sat silently, looking forward. I asked a second time and Vernon continued to sit in silence.

"Vernon, do you know that Jesus loves you and that He knows what you are going through and that He wants to go through it with you? Do you know that, Vernon?"

Vernon turned toward me as tears began to trickle down his face.

"Jesus wants to help," I assured Vernon, "but you have to ask for it. You have to let Him."

Vernon fixed his eyes on mine for what seemed like minutes but was only seconds, before asking with desperation in his voice, "How?"

"Vernon, just tell God that you are sorry for the mess you've made of your life. Tell him that you believe that Jesus died on the cross for your sins and that you want Him to become your Savior and Lord. Ask Jesus Christ to come into your heart. Ask God to be with you from this day on and to strengthen and guide and encourage you for the rest of your life. It's that easy, Vernon."

Vernon bowed his head and silently prayed this simple prayer before bursting into tears as he began to tell me about the skeleton in his past that had tormented him every day of his life.

"My momma was raped." Vernon began to weep. "I was the baby my momma had because of that rape. She tried to kill me before I was born."

"What do you mean, she tried to kill you before you were born?" I asked.

Crying uncontrollably at this point, Vernon continued, "After she found out she was pregnant, she drank a whole bottle of turpentine, hoping it would kill me."

"Father, please help me. Give me the words and the love to share with this one who has never felt the love of his earthly mother or father. Lord, touch him in a way that only you can," I prayed.

"You know, my momma says she loves me, but she treats me different from my brothers and sisters. They all laugh at me and call me weak. I can't take it anymore, I just can't take it. Whenever I try to get help, I always end up talking to strangers like you," Vernon managed to get out before breaking down once again.

"Wait a minute, Vernon, look at me." Vernon's head remained buried between his hands. "I said look at me," I said, my voice growing stern. Startled, Vernon raised his head.

"Vernon, did you just ask Christ into your heart?"

"Yes," he responded.

"Then you know what that makes me? That makes me your brother, Vernon … not a stranger, but your brother in the Lord."

We continued talking for a few more minutes before it was time for Vernon to go. I prayed a short prayer with Vernon before giving him my business card and asking him to call me when he got out of the hospital. Vernon never did have the opportunity to call me.

Later that night as I sat at home, my phone rang. It was my partner Dave.

"Hey, Chris, you remember that crazy guy you were talking to earlier today?"

"Yeah, what about him?"

"He's dead."

A long pause followed as I sat by the phone in disbelief. "What do you mean, he's dead? Vernon was only in his twenties."

"I don't know what happened exactly, but I do know he started having some kind of seizure and ended up dying at the hospital. You had a chance to talk to him, didn't you?" Dave asked.

"Yeah, Dave, I did."

"Well, let's just hope he's in a better place, Chris."

As the initial shock wore off, I began to be overwhelmed with gratitude, appreciation, and love for a Heavenly Father who loved Vernon and me enough to give us both a second chance.

"Yeah, Dave, he's in a better place."

Lesson 22: If the Lord gives second chances to those unworthy, then shouldn't we be willing to do likewise?

LESSON 23
MISTAKES MAKE GREAT TEACHERS

Wait on the LORD; Be of good courage, And He shall strengthen your heart; Wait, I say, on the LORD!

—Psalm 27:14

Have you ever had one of those weeks when you wished you could just stay in bed until it was over? Mine started out routinely enough with me running late for work. I rushed out of the house, realizing I had only fifteen minutes to get to roll call on time.

"Lord," I began to pray as I turned onto the main street, "if possible, I would really appreciate it if you would multiply the fumes left in my gas tank so that I'll have enough gas to get to work and then maybe even enough to get to a gas station. Oh yeah, one more thing, Father ... I would be forever in your debt if you would send a string of green lights my way."

I pulled in at the station with two minutes to spare. *Praise God,* I thought as I quickly double-checked my gear to make sure I hadn't forgotten anything. Bulletproof vest, check; gun belt, check; handcuffs and key, check; flashlight, check; gun, che—. Uh oh. I began to do something just short of panic as I realized I had forgotten my gun at home. There are some things in life that, if forgotten, don't present a problem. Unfortunately, for a police officer, a gun is not one of those things.

"Corporal," I said quietly as I nervously slipped into my supervisor's office. "I have a slight problem tonight."

"What is it, Amos?" the corporal asked.

"Well, sir, it's kind of embarrassing, but, uh ..."

"Out with it, Amos!" my supervisor, who unfortunately was not one of the most sensitive men on the department, interrupted.

"Well, sir, to make a long story short, I forgot my gun at home."

The corporal looked up from the paperwork he was doing and then, with a smile from ear to ear that seemed to spell trouble said, "Don't worry about it, Amos. After roll call, go back home and get it. Okay?"

"Yes, sir," I answered, uncertain about what he had up his sleeve.

"Oh yeah, Amos," the corporal said as I turned to leave his office, "we'll keep this small oversight just between you and me."

I gave one of those halfhearted smiles as I turned to walk away. This was not going to be a good night. I quietly sat in roll call hoping no one would notice that I had forgotten my gun. We stood at attention as the corporal entered the room. He quickly inspected our uniforms before telling us to sit down. *So far, so good,* I thought. Roll call went by as usual. Assignments were given and important information was passed on from the officers we were relieving. Just as I was about to breathe a sigh of relief, it happened.

"Gentlemen," the corporal said, much to my dismay, "I'm going to inspect your guns. Amos, front and center."

I didn't move. He called me to the front a second time.

"Corporal," I hesitantly spoke up, "I don't have a gun to inspect."

The roll call room burst into laughter.

"What do you mean, you don't have a gun to inspect?"

"Well, sir, it's like this. I went to the Andy Griffith School of Policing and was taught I didn't need a gun to protect and serve the public."

"Well, Barney, this ain't Mayberry, so I recommend you run on down the road a piece and pick one up, now, ya hear?"

They say laughter is good medicine. If that's true, it was just what the doctor ordered. I survived the next eight hours, although I did have to endure many a creative joke in which I kept turning up in the punch line. Hey, my week could only get better, or so I thought. I was wrong.

A couple of nights later, I found myself in yet another embarrassing situation. The car sped through the intersection on a red light. *I don't believe this,* I thought. The lady had to know I was behind her. I mean, with the big red-and-blue light and the foot-high letters that say police, how could she not have seen me? *Oh well,* I thought as I activated my lights and siren, eager to pull her over.

"Good evening, ma'am. May I see your license and the registration to your car?"

"Yes, sir," she responded. "Officer, what did I do wrong?"

"Ma'am, what color was the light when you went through that intersection back there?"

"It was yellow"—she paused for a few seconds—"the last time I saw it."

I explained to the woman that the light was red and that I was directly behind her when she went through it. I instructed her to remain in her car as I walked back to mine, intent on writing her a summons. As I reached my car, I waited for traffic to pass before moving to open the door. I reached for the handle and pulled. Nothing happened. I pulled a second time, but got the same result. I looked down and immediately a knot in the pit of my stomach formed as I realized I had locked myself out of my police car.

You might say, "Big deal, so you locked yourself out of your car. Who hasn't?" Unfortunately, my car was running, the red-and-blue lights were flashing, and I was left wondering what to do. Being the "think on your feet" police officer that I am, I slowly turned back toward the car I had stopped.

"Ma'am, tonight's your lucky night. I've had a change of heart. Rather than write you a summons, I'm going to let you go on a warning. Now, slow down and be a little more careful at intersections, okay?"

The woman thanked me before driving off.

Okay, Chris, what are your options? I thought. I could have another unit bring me a spare key. Nah, my week had been embarrassing enough without word of this getting out. My only other option was to get a trusted friend to watch the car while I went door to door in search of a coat hanger.

"One-three-five to one-three-three," I said on my radio.

"One-three-three to one-three-five, go ahead," my friend responded.

"Can I see you in the 3000 block of the boulevard?"

"Ten-four. I'll be to you in five minutes."

As my friend pulled up, I explained the situation to him and asked him to keep an eye on my car. Once he stopped laughing and was able to regain his composure, he agreed. Fortunately, the person in the first apartment I tried had a wire coat hanger I could have. I thanked the person before quickly returning to my car. Within a couple of minutes, I had my door unlocked. I thanked my friend for standing by my car.

"No problem. Maybe you can return the favor sometime."

"Yeah, maybe I can."

As I was about to climb into the car, my friend called out, "Hey, Chris, I'll keep this little mishap just between the two of us."

"Yeah, and I'll be the next chief of police."

He didn't and I wasn't.

Lesson 23: Slow down!

LESSON 24

"THERE AIN'T NO GOD!"

The fool has said in his heart, "There is no God."

—Psalm 14:1a

It is a rare thing in a person's life when he or she experiences firsthand the hostility, unbridled rage, and hatred between the prince of this world, Satan, and the King of Kings, our Lord Jesus Christ. Such was the case on a beautiful Monday evening as my partner and I patrolled Bracy Village on bicycles.

What started out innocently enough as a simple conversation between myself and about seven teenagers quickly turned into a spiritual battle between the supernatural forces of God Almighty and the demonic forces of hell. The spark that ignited this spiritual firefight: the Good News of Jesus Christ.

"Man, there ain't no God, and if there was, He ain't nothin' but a murderer," one of the teens replied.

While laughing, a second said, "You're crazy, man. There ain't no God, and there ain't no heaven and there ain't no hell. When you die, that's it. It's over, man. It's all over."

"Yeah, man, you don't come back to life or any junk like that. When you die, you don't go nowhere but in the ground," a third one chimed in, to support his buddy.

"Have you seen heaven?" the first teen asked me.

83

I sensed at this point that short of a miracle, I was fighting a losing battle in trying to share the Good News of Jesus with this bunch.

"No, I haven't seen heaven with my natural eyes, but I know it is as real a place as this neighborhood you live in."

The group erupted into laughter before a fourth teen asked me if I was afraid to die.

"No, I'm not afraid to die, because I know without a doubt that I'll be welcomed into heaven before this body hits the ground."

"Okay, then give me your gun and I'll smoke you right here, right now. No, I'll give you a chance to call your wife and kids and tell them good-bye—then I'll smoke you."

Again, the group erupted into laughter. My stomach turned, not out of anger or hate, but rather because I felt almost overwhelmed by something very evil, and yet Jesus enabled me to stand my ground.

I guess partly out of disgust, I told them all that they were sadly mistaken if they thought they were in control of their lives.

"Guys, you just don't get it, do you? You come across so big and bad and think you run this park, when in reality you yourselves are being run."

This went over real well with this group.

"Man, you're crazy. Ain't nobody runnin' me," one of the teens responded.

"Yeah, maybe no person is runnin' you, but I'm not talking about people. The fact is that the devil has a hold on you that only Jesus Christ will be able to break."

The first teen quickly countered, "Oh yeah, are you kidding? There ain't no devil in this park. If there is, I want to talk to—"

Before he could finish his sentence, a fourth teen proclaimed with a smirk, "I am the devil!"

"Yeah, he's the devil and this is hell!" another teen cried out in laughter as he pointed to his friend.

I hung my head, not out of shame but rather pity and disgust that so many could be so rebellious toward the only source of true hope they will ever have.

After several minutes of listening to these teens I finally said, "Let me leave you with this one thought, guys. If I am right and each and every one of us will stand before God and have to answer for our actions, then I can promise you this: On that day you will remember every word I have spoken—every word. But more important, God will make sure you remember every insulting and defiant word you have said against Him and the truths of His Word."

The group turned and walked away, continuing to shout and laugh about that "crazy" policeman as they disappeared around a corner. To my surprise, one of the teens stayed behind to talk. Our conversation was brief before he, too, walked away. I couldn't help but think that maybe, just maybe, a seed was planted in the heart of that one teen that may lead him to Jesus Christ.

As my partner and I began to ride down the street, I was looking down, quietly asking God if I had done the right thing or had cast pearls before swine. I began to feel as though I had made a terrible mistake when suddenly out of the corner of my eye I saw something shiny lying in the gutter under a streetlight. I turned, and in disbelief, I saw an old, battered penny. As I bent to pick the penny up, something I had grown accustomed to doing, I reminded myself that it was for the kingdom of God.

Suddenly, I felt the presence of my heavenly Father as He reminded me, "Yes, Chris, that is for my kingdom. You are my kingdom builder, and whether it be an old, battered penny lying on the street or an angry, rebellious teenager standing on the corner, I need you to continue building. Chris, I love you with a love far greater than you know, but guess what? I love them too. You did the right thing. Sometimes building my kingdom is met with tremendous hostility, but you must continue to build. Remember this, my child: the truth will set free only those who accept it. For those who choose to deny it, freedom will be only a dream. As you have seen tonight, to deny my truth is to lead a life of anger, rage, and rebellion toward me and toward my children. But fear not, Chris, for if I am for you, it matters not who is against you."

I thanked God for showing me His love and support, but even more, I was thankful that He reminded me yet again that He is in control of all things.

Lesson 24: God never promised ease and comfort as we work to build His kingdom, but He did promise the grace needed to get the job done.

LESSON 25
"OH YES, THERE IS!"

But I say to you, love your enemies, bless those who curse
you, do good to those who hate you, and pray for those
who spitefully use you and persecute you, that you may
be sons of your Father in heaven; for He makes His sun
rise on the evil and on the good, and sends rain on the
just and on the unjust.

—Matthew 5:44–45

The group turned and walked away, continuing to shout and laugh
about that "crazy" policeman as they disappeared around a corner.
To my surprise, one of the teens stayed behind to talk. Our conversation
was brief before he, too, walked away. I couldn't help but think that
maybe, just maybe, a seed was planted in the heart of that one teen that
may lead him to Jesus Christ.

The image in my mind of that evening faded over time, as did
the anger I felt as those teens, deeply lost in sin, took turns verbally
assaulting my Savior and Lord. God had given me a peace concerning
the actions I took that night, yet I was still left asking God, "For what
purpose did I have to stand by, doing nothing as these teens attacked
you? I don't understand, Father." God most assuredly did.

Almost one year later to the day I found myself back in the same
neighborhood dealing with the same group of teens, only this time

the reason was far more serious. One of the teens had bought a gun and decided he would take it outside to see if it worked. He was happy to discover the gun worked as he fired five rounds into the ground. Unfortunately for him, his neighbor's telephone worked as well, and she immediately dialed 911.

My partner and I arrived on the scene a short time later. Within a couple of minutes we had recovered the gun and arrested the shooter. As I sat, looking into my rearview mirror at the young man slouched down in the backseat of my police car, I felt led to ask, "Have I ever talked to you before, Michael?"

"Yes, sir, you have," he replied respectfully.

"When?"

"You talked to me and my friends about the Bible last year."

My mind raced back to that night, which I now pictured as clearly as if it had just happened yesterday.

"Michael, were you the one who stayed behind when the others walked off?"

"Yes, sir," he answered quietly.

"Why didn't you leave with your friends? Why did you stay around?" I couldn't help but ask.

"I guess it was because I wanted to hear what you had to say, sir." *Really,* I thought. At the time it sure hadn't seemed to me like anyone cared about what I had to say. I immediately began my favorite and most commonly used prayer: "Father, help!"

I stopped believing in coincidences a long time ago, and I knew God had something planned for Michael this day.

"Father, may I not get in the way of your plans for Michael. Give me Your words, Father, and give me Your wisdom," I silently prayed as I turned around in my seat and looked into Michael's desperate eyes.

"Michael, do you remember what I said that evening?"

"Yes," he answered with certainty.

"Well, there is more I think you ought to know, and this may be the day you hear it."

Michael nodded in agreement as we pulled away from the street corner and began the ride to the station.

A few minutes later we found ourselves sitting in a small room, face-to-face.

I learned a great deal about Michael as we talked about his life at home and school. He was the weak one of the group. He was the one who was most easily intimidated and taken advantage of. He was the one who caved in to peer pressure and did things he'd regret later, like shooting a gun into the ground or stealing a car. He was the one who was always trying to prove his manhood to his friends but never succeeded. He was, in short, the outcast.

"Michael," I began to say reassuringly, "the void you feel in your life—you know, the one you've been trying to fill with your friends' approval and acceptance—can be filled by only one person. Do you know who I'm talking about?"

Michael hesitated a few seconds before lifting his head and staring directly into my eyes. "Jesus. That person is Jesus, isn't it?"

I smiled as I nodded in agreement. "Michael, do you want to meet Jesus?"

"Yes, sir, I do. Will you help me?"

I spent the next several minutes sharing the Good News of Jesus Christ with this young man. Once finished, I grabbed Michael's hand and began to lead him in a sinner's prayer.

As we finished praying with heads still bowed, I was reminded of the question I had raised months earlier: "For what purpose did I have to sit by, doing nothing as these teens attacked you? I don't understand, Father."

I could sense God lovingly reply, "For what purpose, you asked? Chris, open your eyes."

As I opened my eyes, there sat Michael smiling with tears streaming down his face.

"Thank you, Father, thank you."

Lesson 25: The love of a kingdom builder must be vulnerable to foe as well as friend. If it is, God will do mighty things.

LESSON 26
WHY?

Trust in the LORD with all your heart, and lean not on your own understanding; in all your ways acknowledge Him, and He shall direct your paths.

—Proverbs 3:5–6

The stage had been set that cold, February night for a tragedy that few, if any, of the officers on the scene were really prepared for. The call went out as a "violent domestic" involving a man with a gun. The first officers on the scene quickly realized that what may have begun as a "domestic" had escalated into a barricaded gunman with three hostages.

Immediately the officers called for backup, and from the other side of the city I listened to my police radio, unable to do anything but pray for all those involved as the nightmare unfolded.

Officer 1: I've got the south side of the house covered, but I need someone to take the back and north sides.

Officer 2: I'll take the back.

Officer 3: I'll take the north side.

Officer 1: Has the SWAT team been called out?

Supervisor: The SWAT team and the hostage negotiation team have both been called out. They should be here in ten minutes. Everybody just hold your positions. If you see any movement inside the house, speak up.

Officer 1: He's coming out the side door! He has a gun! He has a gun!

Officer 2: Does he have the hostages?

Officer 1: He has a gun!

Supervisor: Hold your fire.

Officer 2: Does he have the hostages? Where are the hostages?

Officer 4: Watch your line of fire.

Officer 1: He's gone back inside. He has gone back inside.

Supervisor: Everybody hold your positions; we don't want to spook him.

(Ten seconds pass before shots are heard coming from inside the house.)

Officer 1: He's shooting inside the house!

Officer 2: Radio, advise the field commander that multiple shots have been fired inside the house.

(The sound of gunfire is immediately followed by the gunman running out the side door of the two-story home.)

Officer 1: He's coming out the side door! He's got a gun!

(A mic is keyed. Several gunshots are heard being fired in the background.)

Officer 1: Suspect has been hit. He's down! He's down!

Officer 4: Suspect is in custody. Radio, advise the paramedics that the suspect has been shot in the chest.

(With the suspect in custody, the officers turn their attention to the house. They enter cautiously, not knowing if a second gunman is inside.)

Officer 1: *(Yelling is heard in the background)* Get me a paramedic, radio—I need a paramedic now!

Officer 3: Dispatcher, we need paramedics now … Three victims, radio … All three have received gunshot wounds to the head.

Officer 1: Code Red! I need a paramedic!

Dispatcher: What are the conditions of the victims?

Officer 4: All three have gunshot wounds to the head. Where are those paramedics?

Supervisor: They are pulling up now.

Officer 1: We need three paramedics! We need three!

(Radio is silent for several minutes.)

Supervisor: Dispatcher, contact homicide. We need investigators to respond.

Officers entered the house immediately after the gunman was shot and killed. They found three victims, all of whom had been shot in the head. Two of the three victims died inside the house. The third, a woman in her late fifties, survived.

That night, street-toughened cops cried: SWAT team members and hostage negotiators, supervisors and patrolmen alike. Men and women accustomed to dealing with violence and death cried. Many of them went home and awakened their children, cradling them tightly in their arms, not wanting to let go.

It was a long time before those officers were able to put that tragic night behind them and move on. The motive for the shooting died that night with the gunman. The sight of a precious little five-year-old girl lying dead in a pool of blood would not.

Lesson 26: As Christians, may we have the wisdom to realize that we do not always know the reason why, and the faith to believe that God does.

LESSON 27
WHO'S IN CONTROL?

And I heard a loud voice from heaven saying, "Behold, the tabernacle of God is with men, and He will dwell with them, and they shall be His people. God Himself will be with them and be their God. And God will wipe away every tear from their eyes; there shall be no more death, nor sorrow, nor crying. There shall be no more pain, for the former things have passed away."

—Revelation 21:3–4

Who is in control of this world anyway? I feel as if over the last seventy-two hours I have been staring into the cold, callous eyes of Satan himself. If pride truly goes before the fall, then I can't help but think Satan's final fall is close at hand. I feel as if Satan is defiantly flaunting the control and power he still exercises over this world and those who inhabit it. Is Satan making his last act of defiance before an all-powerful God swoops down on him as an eagle swoops down on its unsuspecting prey?

In a week's time, I have seen humanity at its worst. I have witnessed the tearful separation of five young, neglected children from their crack-addicted mother. I responded to the brutal beating of an out of town convention attendee by a group of bat-wielding juvenile thugs. I listened to my police radio in disbelief as an enraged father shot and killed his wife and five-year-old daughter before being killed himself in a hail of police gunfire. The children, the convention attendee, the mother, and her five-year-old daughter all had one thing in common: innocence.

Satan must have looked on with great joy as these lives were torn apart, maimed, and destroyed. The pain and the suffering of these victims must surely have brought a smile to Satan's face, yet I believe Satan experienced much the same sense of joy and exhilaration nearly two thousand years ago. This time the innocent victim was not a little girl or a convention attendee from out of town, but rather Jesus Christ Himself.

As Jesus Christ began to experience the excruciating death by crucifixion, Satan must have truly felt as if he were finally in total control of the world and all those who lived within it. The pleasure he experienced while watching the divine blood of God Incarnate stream down the sides of that cross before forming a bloody muddy mess at its base must have been overwhelming. And yet, like so many of Satan's victories now, it was proven to be short lived.

True, for a short while Satan appeared to have been the victor, yet the very victory he claimed was actually the fatal blow to all that he had hoped to be and do. Can it be that the attacks and temporary victories that Satan appears to be enjoying now are simply the desperate acts of a defeated foe frantically trying to regain that which he lost on a hill called Calvary? I have seen Satan strike again and again, and I know he will continue to do so until his appointed time has come.

How am I to deal with the pain, suffering, and injustice that so many experience day after day in a seemingly never-ending cycle? How? I ask, and then, Father, you remind me that the time is coming when you "will wipe every tear from their eyes. There will be no more death or mourning or crying or pain, for the old order of things has passed away."

To those suffering who do not know Jesus I say, "Open your heart to the only one who can make sense of what you are going through, Jesus Christ." To those suffering who do know Jesus I say, "Stand fast, friend. The tear you shed today may well be your very last for all eternity."

Lesson 27: Suffering may not be a choice. Suffering alone is.

LESSON 28
HELP FROM THE HOMELESS

And He looked up and saw the rich putting their gifts into the treasury, and He saw also a certain poor widow putting in two mites. So He said, "Truly I say to you that this poor widow has put in more than all; for all these out of their abundance have put in offerings for God, but she out of her poverty put in all the livelihood that she had."

—Luke 21: 1–4

Many walk past, avoiding them if possible, ignoring them if not. Their lives consist of a mundane routine mixed with brief moments of fear that most know nothing of. For many, their appearance does not change for days, even weeks at a time. They are viewed as a burden to society with little if anything to offer in exchange for a hot sandwich or bowl of soup. They have been labeled as vagrants or bums in times past, but now they are simply known as the homeless, and they are everywhere.

You may have passed one holding a sign offering to work in exchange for food. Another may have asked you for some spare change as you walked to lunch. Still another may have offered to wash your car or shop windows, or some other hustle, in exchange for money or food. And then there are those who spend day after day on the street corner or a park bench when the weather is good, in the city library when it is not. Some are homeless by choice, whereas many others are not. All are created in the image of God, and for that reason alone, they are priceless.

His name was Michael. His mere appearance struck fear or disgust in many people. He was unkempt, as are many of those living on the streets. He did wash up at the local bus station occasionally. The years of living on the street, or in Michael's case, under a bridge, showed on his hollow face. Michael's smile had everything a person could want with the exception of teeth. He had a gap about five teeth wide in the dead center of his mouth. His hair was brown and coarse, the result of washing it only once a week. Michael spoke with a terrible lisp that made it difficult to understand him. This did nothing but further alienate him from those around him, as did the nearly inch-long whiskers that covered portions of his face.

At one time Michael was a computer consultant with a nice home, but that seemed like a lifetime ago. After losing his job and house, Michael eventually came to call the streets home.

One day while I was talking to Michael in a local convenience store, a stranger walked through the doors. It was obvious that the man was new to the area and, like Michael, called the streets his home.

"I remember being in as bad a shape as that guy," Michael commented as he watched the stranger clean his face with a napkin. "I remember what it was like to arrive in a new city with no money, no friends, no food—with nothing, absolutely nothing." I wondered what kind of shape Michael thought he was in now.

Without hesitating, Michael approached the stranger and offered to buy him a drink and a sandwich, because, as Michael said, "Friend, it looks like you need it." I watched in amazement as Michael reached into his pocket and pulled out a handful of change, most of which went to pay for the stranger's meal.

I wished Michael well that day before climbing into my police car and driving away. I began to think of the gifts God had given me, gifts I had taken for granted for far too long: a beautiful wife, three healthy kids, a nice home, and on and on the list went. Tears began to form in my eyes as I looked at Michael, a man giving not out of great wealth, but out of utter poverty, expecting nothing in return. It was then that this homeless, unkempt, toothless man painted one of the clearest, most beautiful portraits of the love of Jesus Christ that I had ever seen.

Does God bless this kind of giving? A few days later another stranger gave Michael twenty dollars and a sleeping bag. Then again, maybe—just maybe—it wasn't a stranger after all.

Thanks, Michael.

Lesson 28: Giving is admirable. Sacrificial giving is Christ-like. Which do you want to be?

LESSON 29
TRUST ME, SON; JUST TRUST ME

You are of your father the devil, and the desires of your father you want to do. He was a murderer from the beginning, and does not stand in the truth, because there is no truth in him. When he speaks a lie, he speaks from his own resources, for he is a liar and the father of it.

—John 8:44

"**B**ut sir, I know I shot the targets in the proper order. I did exactly what you told me to do in the order you told me to do it," the officer said adamantly.

"Son, I followed you through the course, and you shot the second series of targets out of sequence," the range sergeant replied.

"But ..."

"But nothing, son, I saw you. Here, let me lead you through the course step by step, and I'll show you what you did. Trust me, son; just trust me."

With those words our range sergeant put his arm around the confused police officer before walking him through the course. I must admit, the young officer wasn't the only policeman confused by what Sergeant Tosk was saying—so was I. I scored the targets as the officer went through the course initially, and the officer was right. He shot the targets in the proper sequence, and he got a perfect score in the process.

I tried to tell Sergeant Tosk that he was mistaken, but he wanted to hear none of that, so I was left with simply watching in amazement as our dearly beloved Sergeant Tosk worked his magic on this young officer.

"Now, son, you approached this target okay. You put two rounds in the target on the left and then two in the target on the right. So far, so good. Any questions?"

The young officer had none as he concentrated on the sergeant's every word.

"You removed your finger from the trigger before running up to this barricade. So far, textbook." Sergeant Tosk, with his arm around the confused officer, the two ran up to the next barricade. "Now, this is when things got ugly. Do you see those three targets down there?"

"Yes, sir," the officer replied.

"Good! You were supposed to put two rounds in the middle target, two in the right, and then two in the left, right?"

"Yes, sir, but I thought I—"

"That's your problem, son. You were thinking instead of shooting," Sergeant Tosk interrupted. "You put two rounds in the left, two in the middle, then two in the right—out of sequence, son. That means all six rounds are counted as misses. You failed, but don't worry about it. Just reload and run through it again."

The now bewildered officer walked away scratching his head. He turned back toward Tosk. "Sarge, I'll get it right this time."

"I know you will, son," Sergeant Tosk replied reassuringly.

As the officer headed back to the starting line to reshoot the course, Sergeant Tosk winked at me and with a wily grin from ear to ear, triumphantly declared, "I got another one."

Lesson 29: Do not accept the lies of Satan no matter how convincing they may sound.

LESSON 30
PROMISES

... who, contrary to hope, in hope believed, so that he became the father of many nations, according to what was spoken, "So shall your descendants be." And not being weak in faith, he did not consider his own body, already dead (since he was about a hundred years old), and the deadness of Sarah's womb. He did not waver at the promise of God through unbelief, but was strengthened in faith, giving glory to God, and being fully convinced that what He had promised He was also able to perform.

—Romans 4:18–21

"That will be $2.83," the cashier said after ringing up my lunch order.

My partner Gary was standing at the next register. He looked toward me and smiled before turning to the woman taking his order. "I'll get the same thing he did."

The cashier pressed a few buttons on the register. "That will be $4.78."

"Wait a minute. I got the same thing he did," Gary responded, somewhat surprised, "and his was only $2.83."

Actually, Gary was a little more than somewhat surprised. He had only five dollars on him, and his truck was on empty.

"Either I eat or my truck does," Gary had informed me earlier, "and it is probably more important that my truck does if I'm going to make it home after work."

"Gary, trust me, this place gives us a break when we eat inside," I had assured him. "We can eat for under three bucks, I promise. After all, I only have three dollars." Reluctantly Gary agreed to eat. I looked at the woman who rang up Gary's order. I noticed that her name tag said "trainee" on it. *Uh oh, that's not good,* I thought.

"I forgot to tell you, Nancy. The police get a discount when they eat inside, but, oh well, it's too late now," my cashier told the trainee as they both began to chuckle.

Out of the corner of my eye I saw smoke rising into the air. At first, I thought it was rising off the grill behind the counter. With a closer glance, I saw it was actually coming from Gary's forehead.

I quietly sat down with my tray, as did Gary directly across from me. Not wanting to upset Gary any more than he already was, I remained silent, staring at my food. After a couple of minutes of tension-filled silence, I headed for the bathroom. Once inside, I turned on the water and the hand blow dryer. Confident that Gary would not be able to hear, I erupted into an uncontrollable, gut-splitting laughter that brought tears to my eyes. A few minutes later, I returned to our table, relieved that I had gotten the laughter out of my system.

"So, Gary, how's lunch?" He didn't see the humor in my question.

"If you need a ride home after work—" Before I could finish, the manager walked up to our table.

"I'm sorry, Officer. Our trainee didn't know about your discount. Here is the rest of your change." He handed Gary a couple of dollars.

Gary finished his meal before the two of us began to get up.

"See, Gary, I told you we could eat for under three bucks."

Lesson 30: The promises of God are true, even when our circumstances suggest otherwise.

LESSON 31
SODOM, USA

For God so loved the world that He gave His only begotten
Son, that whoever believes in Him should not perish but
have everlasting life.

—John 3:16

The fireworks burst in the muggy, starlit June sky as thousands of
people turned their eyes skyward to witness an explosive display of
lights and colors that was, in a word, awesome. The fireworks display was
the climax of a three-day festival in which tens of thousands of people
had made their way to the waterfront to celebrate. The spectators, most
of whom fought crowds and traffic, were not disappointed as the show
went off without a hitch. I had seen fireworks displays in the past, but
none were as captivating as this.

The fireworks themselves were spectacular in both quantity and
quality. The musical theme that accompanied the show was patriotic
and upbeat. Like those around me, I was caught up in the excitement
that seemed to feed off of every exploding display of color. It was as if
for a split second, we were all one great big, happy family: white and
black, rich and poor, young and old, all with one purpose and one
desire—to celebrate!

Suddenly, it was as if a spiritual alarm went off in my head signifying,
The party's over! The words to the song quickly caught my attention.

"God bless America, land that I love. Stand beside her, and guide her ..." As this beautiful anthem was playing in the background and fireworks were exploding overhead, something caught my eye. I turned and saw a man staggering over to the bathroom, so drunk he could hardly stay on his feet. I then noticed two more men involved in an argument that was about to turn into a fistfight. Both men were drunk. Oh, the fireworks were still exploding overhead, but that hardly seemed to matter now as my eyes were opened to a virtual sea of drunks. My indignation grew as I saw yet another group of men and women walk past, each carrying a stack of about fifteen empty beer cups, one inside the other, as if they were proudly proclaiming to the world, "I drank fifteen beers and can still walk!" The electricity I had experienced just minutes earlier was quickly replaced by anger and disgust. One thought began to occupy my mind: *How dare you! How dare you ask for God's blessings on this beerfest!*

I turned to my partner. "Dave, this is crazy. This is absolutely crazy. I don't know what God they expect to look down on this drunk-fest and bless it, but I can promise you this: it certainly isn't my God."

A group of people openly mocking God Almighty caught my attention. Apparently I wasn't the only one listening to the lyrics of the songs being played. "God," I prayed silently, "how dare they even call on your name. Father, how can you put up with this? With one word you could remove this, this sin-infested celebration from the face of the earth. Why don't you, Father? Why?"

As my anger began to grow and my sense of self-righteousness began to swell, God quietly and lovingly reminded me of my own fourteen-year addiction to pornography and the patience, love, and grace He had exercised in dealing with me. I quietly dropped my head, ashamed of my own puffed-up demonstration of holiness.

"My child," I sensed God lovingly continuing, "as for removing this place from the face of the earth with a single word, you're right ... I can, but I'm not going to. Not now, not yet. No, before I remove the unsaved sinner, I will remove you and all those who have been born again of my grace. Until that time, you must love them as I have loved you. Do not allow their sin to harden your heart. No, you must guard against that. Their sin, their contempt for me— allow it to break your heart as it does mine. If I am to love them through you, it will be through your brokenness, and, my child, that is exactly what I will do."

Lesson 31: Satan despises the drunkard. God reaches out to the drunkard while despising the drink. Whose child are you?

LESSON 32
"IT'S GOING TO TAKE A MIRACLE"

Now after the two days He departed from there and went to Galilee. For Jesus Himself testified that a prophet has no honor in his own country.

—John 11:43–44

My words were full of gloom and doom as I answered the question posed to me by my pastor.

"Chris, as a police officer, do you think things have gotten worse over the last five years?"

"Pastor, I've been doing police work for a long time, and from what I've seen, the answer is yes. To be truthful, things have gone from bad to worse. The traditional family—dad, mom, and the kids—is hard to find where I work. What little trust and respect for authority there is seems to be on the decline, and I'm not just talking about for the police. Pastor, the police, the courts, the schools, the church—they are all, for the most part, looked on with suspicion, contempt, and in many cases, just plain disgust by the general public."

I continued painting a picture of gloom and doom with one example after another before ending with this: "Pastor, unless God intervenes in a miraculous way, I just don't see a whole lot of hope on the horizon."

Pastor Smith dropped his head before raising it ever so slowly. "Chris, we still have to keep praying … and trying." I shook my head halfheartedly before telling him good-bye and heading for work.

Within an hour, I found myself riding my police mountain bike through one of the very areas I had written off as hopeless. I saw a group of men a couple of blocks up the street who appeared to be engaged in a drug deal. I shifted to a higher gear as my legs began to pump harder. My heartbeat quickened as I concentrated all my attention on the group. While still a block away I was spotted, someone shouted, "Five-oh," the street name for the police, and the group quickly dispersed.

Okay, Chris, who has the drugs? I asked myself as I rode up to the dispersing group. "The tank top—go after the guy in the tank top," something told me.

"Hey! Hold up a second," I called out to the man wearing the white tank top and blue jeans.

He turned. "Who, me?"

"Yeah, you," I answered. I asked for his identification before explaining why I had stopped him.

"Officer, I'm clean. I was just walking through," the young man countered.

Suddenly, it was as if my suspicions didn't matter. I mean, it was as if my drug hunch wasn't my reason for stopping Kenny.

"Kenny," I felt led to ask for no logical reason, "do you read your Bible?"

He looked up at me, caught off guard by the question. "Not as much as I should."

"It has a lot to say about staying out of trouble. Like 'Bad company corrupts moral character,' among other things."

Kenny began to open up a little bit about his problems. The more we spoke about the Lord, the greater the sense of hunger I could see in Kenny's eyes. After what seemed like just a couple of minutes, but was actually an hour, I extended my hand to Kenny. He grabbed it eagerly.

"Kenny, God wants you to stop running and come to Him with your arms extended toward the sky."

"What do you mean?" he interrupted.

"I mean God wants you to give up, to quit, to surrender. When I go to arrest a person who poses a threat to me, I ask him to get his hands up in the air. Do you know why?" Kenny nodded.

"I do it for four reasons. First, it means he no longer poses as great a threat as he did before. Second, it shows me that he is willing to do what I tell him to. Third, it puts him in a position where he is off balance. He has lost whatever physical advantage he may have had. And finally, he is vulnerable with his hands up in the air. He can't protect himself; he's totally exposed. Kenny, that is exactly what God wants you to do: surrender to Him, obey His instructions, stop relying on yourself—your own strength, wisdom, and determination—and finally, be open, be vulnerable to Him."

We spoke for a few more minutes before I turned to leave. As I was riding through the courtyard, I remembered my earlier conversation with Pastor Smith.

"Pastor, unless God intervenes in a miraculous way, I just don't see any hope."

"Chris," I quietly sensed God call, "who made you the giver and taker of hope?"

Feeling about an inch tall, I realized that I had questioned God's ability to move among these men and women. God didn't leave me wallowing in self-pity for long. He added lovingly, "My child, you spoke of a miracle earlier. Guess what? You are that miracle. You and every man, woman, and child who has accepted Christ as their Savior and Lord. Chris, you are my Lazarus. You are the miracle through which I desire to work. If I am to use you, my child, you cannot—you must not—lose hope."

The next day I pulled Pastor Smith to the side after the morning worship service, eager to tell him about my experience.

"Pastor," I began, "I was wrong, dead wrong! Hope is alive and well!"

Lesson 32: The next time you say it's going to take a miracle, remember, if you are a Christian, that you are one.

LESSON 33
FAIRY TALES

For the message of the cross is foolishness to those who are perishing, but to us who are being saved it is the power of God.

—1 Corinthians 1:18

"That stuff is a fairy tale. It doesn't work in life. Not in the real world. It's just a fairy tale, man, a fairy tale."

The "stuff" being referred to was the gospel of Jesus Christ, and the one making the statement was a middle-aged man named Floyd Brown. To Floyd's dismay, my partner and I nabbed him just seconds after he bought a small bag of crack cocaine. Floyd took one look at us and did what any levelheaded cocaine addict would do. He swallowed the bag.

Floyd managed to beat the system by swallowing the evidence that would have convicted him in court. Ironically, even though we had no charges on Floyd, we still had a bit of a problem.

"So, let me get this straight," my partner Dave asked. "We have to babysit Brown for four hours while he sits in the emergency room for observation."

"Yep, you got it," I answered.

"This is crazy! I can't charge him but I can babysit him. What's wrong with this picture?" Dave responded, more than a little ticked off by what was happening.

"What do you mean, it's fairy tale stuff, Floyd?" I asked as I found myself sitting on a stool next to his hospital bed.

"Well, it sounds good and well, but people can't live like that, man. I mean, it doesn't work when you are alone on the streets with no money and driven by a heroin or crack addiction."

"You are right about life on the streets. The streets are cold and callous and just don't care. It is hard, Floyd, but—" I managed to say before he interrupted me.

"But nothing, man—it doesn't work! You may believe in all that, and I respect that, but I don't."

"Are you happy, Floyd?" I asked.

"What do you think?"

"I'm serious: are you happy?"

"Man, I haven't been happy since I was a junior in high school. That was over twenty years ago." Tears began to form in Floyd's rugged, street-weary eyes. "You know, I used to be happy a long time ago, but I went to 'Nam and started to use drugs, and my life has been a living hell ever since."

For the next three and a half hours I found myself listening to yet another man who had lost all hope of conquering his addiction to drugs. As I tried to explain the message of hope and deliverance found in Jesus, I began to realize why Floyd had opposed it so strongly at the start.

"My mother is a Christian, and I saw how she gave to those on the street that she said had less than us. Man, nobody had less than us. We lived in poverty, but she still gave away what little she had. She'd tell us that we were responsible to look out for others and she did that all her life, but she ain't got nothin' to show for it now—nothin'. I mean, we struggled to get by my whole life and my momma is still struggling to get by now. For what, man? For what? Because that's what Jesus said? What did my momma ever get for all those years she did without? Thanks, but no thanks. That stuff doesn't work, and you can keep it."

"Tell me if I'm wrong, Floyd, but I don't think I will be. I've never met your momma, but just from listening to you I would say your momma is a lady with an unshakeable faith in God. My guess is she has a love for others and life that is tough to explain. She is content and thankful for what little she has. She would literally give you the coat off her back if you needed it or food off her table. Am I right?" I did not need a verbal answer. Floyd began to nod in agreement, and a smile broke out on his street-hardened face for the first time.

"You asked what she has to show for it, and I'll tell you what she has, Floyd. She has a peace that transcends understanding. She has a joy in her heart that can't be taken away. And, she has a great excitement and anticipation as she nears the end of this life and the beginning of the next. You say she has nothing, Floyd, but I'll tell you something. Your momma has made a decision to invest in the eternal treasures of heaven, and I can promise you she won't be disappointed."

Floyd quietly hung his head before sharing with me about the time he was nearly killed in an automobile accident a few years earlier but had miraculously survived.

"I guess that's something else your momma has for believing in 'fairy tales,'" I said.

"What's that?" Floyd asked.

"A son who is alive today because of her prayers."

"What do you mean?"

"I mean your momma has got to be a woman of prayer."

"She is, I know that," he answered with certainty.

"Yeah, and because she loved you enough to pray for you as only a mother could, you were spared during that accident. Now, whether or not you consider your life something to show for your momma's faith really doesn't matter, Floyd. Your momma knows she has the life of her baby because God heard and answered her prayers."

The hours seemed to fly by as we sat talking until finally it was time for Floyd to be released from the hospital. As I turned to leave, Floyd called out my name. "Amos!"

"Yeah, Floyd?" I answered.

"I'd appreciate it if you would say a little prayer for me."

"Yeah, Floyd, I will."

"Oh, yeah, one more thing. You know ... I guess ... I mean, it's not a fairy tale. I mean, Jesus and the cross and what you and my momma believe, it's real. It really is real."

"Yeah, Floyd, it is," I responded with a grin.

Lesson 33: To accept the truth of God and do as He says is to live eternally "happily ever after."

LESSON 34
TRUE OR FALSE

A good tree cannot bear bad fruit, nor can a bad tree bear good fruit. Every tree that does not bear good fruit is cut down and thrown into the fire. Therefore by their fruits you will know them.

—Matthew 7:18–20

The call, "man with a gun," was pretty common, considering the location. The alleged gun-wielding individual turned out to be seventeen-year-old Ernest Wilson—E for short. Apparently, E had decided to point a gun at one of his neighbors. Much to E's surprise, the neighbor, rather than cowering in fear, came real close to taking the weapon and shooting E with his own gun. By the time we arrived, the gun, predictably, had disappeared.

E was immediately put in the back of our police car while the situation was being investigated. I sat with E for a long time and had an opportunity to look inside the mind of a young man who will be fortunate if he lives to see his twenty-fifth birthday.

You see, E did not have a very good track record. By the ripe old age of seventeen, he had already been shot once as well as arrested and sent upstate to the maximum-security juvenile detention center for robbery, malicious wounding, and several other charges. All in all, E was on the fast track to either the state penitentiary or the local cemetery.

"I want my lawyer," E demanded immediately. "This ain't right, man. This ain't right. What are you going to do to me now, man? Beat me like Rodney King?"

I listened quietly, not saying a thing in return.

Shortly after his outburst as he and I sat alone in the car, he turned to me and said, "You are different, I can tell."

"Oh, I am," I replied.

"Yeah, I can tell you don't go around harassing people, like your partner does."

"I tell you what I think," I responded. "I think you are a good actor. I think you had a gun and you know you had a gun."

E shook his head and mumbled something under his breath about how the white man was keeping him down.

"What do you know about white and black?" I asked.

"Enough."

I persisted. "Oh, yeah, who taught you? My guess is the boys in your posse."

"You don't want to know," E countered.

"No, tell me. I really want to know. Who taught you?"

E looked me in the eyes and replied, "Allah."

I looked E in the eyes and said, "Allah? Who's Allah? You Muslim?"

"My God is black. No, I'm not Muslim, I'm a five percenter."

I asked E what a five percenter was. He really had no idea. I began to share with him that I too have a God, only my God is not concerned with color or race or financial status. My God looks at the heart and the motives of the heart, and my God will judge each man according to what he has or has not done.

We sat silently in the car for a few minutes before I asked E, "What did you do with the gun?"

"What gun? I don't know what you're talking about. I didn't have no gun."

I looked E in the eyes again and said, "You are lying. You had a gun and pointed it at the head of another man, and that is the reason you are sitting in the back of my car." I didn't say anything for a few seconds and then said, "I guess Allah believes in lying."

"Yeah," E replied quietly.

"What?" I asked.

"I guess he does," E answered.

Again, a few minutes passed before I asked, "How do you like serving a God that believes in lying? I mean, if it were me, I'd be afraid he'd be telling me to do A, B, and C to get to heaven, and then when I die, he'd say, 'Sorry, I lied. You're going to hell.'"

E thought about it for a couple of seconds before answering, "Yeah, I guess he could be doing that."

I began to ask Earnest about his arrest record, which he shared openly and even boastfully. Once again I asked, "So tell me, does Allah believe in robbing people, beating people, and selling drugs?"

Once again E quietly answered, "Yeah, I guess so."

Several more minutes passed before I asked, "Do you believe in hell?"

"Yeah, I believe in hell."

"Who does Allah send to hell?" I asked.

"Bad people," he answered.

"So, I guess all those people who don't steal, rob, murder, and lie will be going to hell—I mean, since Allah believes in doing all those things, right?"

This was the first time I could sense that Ernest was disturbed outwardly and inwardly. "Well ... yeah, I guess so. I mean, I don't know, man—you said it."

I looked into eyes filled with uncertainty as I said, "Ernest, this may seem hard for you to believe, but God loves you. I know in the parks, love is a sign of weakness and vulnerability, but—"

"No, I don't think it's a sign of weakness," Ernest interrupted.

I continued, "I bet nine out of every ten of your buddies have never experienced the love of their father, so how can they accept the fact that they have a heavenly Father who loves them? But I am here to tell you that He does, Ernest."

I left it at that. I think E had a lot to think about, and it was my prayer that he would do just that. He asked me if he was going to be locked up. I told him I didn't know, but that God loved him enough to lock him up if that's what it took to make him think about our conversation. E wasn't real impressed with that line of reasoning. "You let me out right now and ask me in front of all my boys what I'll do with Jesus, and I'll tell you," he said.

"Ernest, you don't have to prove anything to me or to your boys. The decision you make is between you and God."

E turned his attention to his boys, who by this time had gathered next to my police car. He attempted to mouth a message to his posse. After trying it unsuccessfully for a couple of minutes, he yelled out, "I'm going to get that boy that turned me in. I'm going to mess him up."

I thought to myself, *Another life wasted, another soul lost,* yet then, to my surprise, E turned to me and asked if I had a number. I handed him my business card. E looked up at me as he was being turned over to his mother and said, "Thanks, sir. I'll call you."

I'm still waiting for E's call.

Lesson 34: You think it is hard being a Christian. Try following a "god" who lies.

LESSON 35
HONESTY IS THE BEST POLICY

For we must all appear before the judgment seat of Christ, that each one may receive the things done in the body, according to what he has done, whether good or bad.

—2 Corinthians 5:10

Things weren't going well for Roderick Irwin. I had just finished testifying to the judge about the four-inch steak knife I had found concealed in Roderick's jacket. You might think that carrying a steak knife is no big deal. In one's house it's not, but carrying one hidden in one's jacket while one is trespassing is not only a big deal, but against the law. Such was the case for Roderick. After my testimony, the judge lowered his glasses and began to write on the arrest warrant in front of him. He glanced toward Roderick. "Mr. Irwin, do you have anything to say?"

"No sir, Your Honor," Roderick answered.

"The court finds you guilty. That will be a one-hundred-dollar fine and thirty days in the city jail. Go with the deputy."

About that time Roderick turned three shades of white before regaining his composure. "Your Honor, my ... uh ... my momma has heart problems, and I'm the only one home to care for her. Can you please suspend my time, sir?"

The realization that he was being locked up came crashing over Roderick, and beads of sweat began to form on his forehead. "I've never ... uh ... done anything like this before, Judge," he continued. "Your Honor, I'm a nice guy. I wasn't going to hurt anybody with that knife. Please, Judge, suspend my time."

The judge told Roderick he would consider suspending his sentence after he looked at his record. Fortunately, I had a copy—a very thick copy—of Roderick's previous run-ins with the law. I handed Roderick's record to the judge, and he began to read through it.

"Why were you in the penitentiary in New York?"

"Judge, I never did any time in New York," Roderick answered.

"Is that so, Mr. Irwin? What about this robbery conviction you had three years ago?" the judge countered.

"Oh, uh, that, Judge, was thrown out in court."

"Thrown out was it, Mr. Irwin. It looks to me like you were convicted of robbery and are now on probation as a result."

"I was on probation, Judge, but I'm off now."

"You're off supervised probation, but you are on unsupervised probation and will be for three more years."

Roderick began to realize his situation was going from bad to worse, when to my surprise he turned toward me and quietly muttered, "Help me out, Officer, help me out. You know me. I'm a good guy. I ain't going to hurt anybody. Help me out."

"Roderick," I quietly muttered back, "stop lying to the judge."

"So, Mr. Irwin, about this probation, are you or are you not on unsupervised probation?"

"Well, I used to, uh, yes, Judge, I am."

"Mr. Irwin, your record is terrible. That will be a one-hundred-dollar fine and thirty days in jail. Go with the deputy."

Roderick dropped his head before being led out of the courtroom just two days before Christmas.

Lesson 35: To deny the truth of Jesus Christ is a crime punishable by being sentenced to eternity in hell.

LESSON 36
DEADLY COLD

But a certain Samaritan, as he journeyed, came where he was. And when he saw him, he had compassion. So he went to him and bandaged his wounds, pouring on oil and wine; and he set him on his own animal, brought him to an inn, and took care of him.

—Luke 10:33–34

"That guy doesn't look too good," my partner said as we drove past an elderly man sitting in a chair in front of an old boarded-up gas station that had long since gone out of business.

"Well, let's take a closer look." We turned around and headed back toward the gas station.

As we pulled into the lot, I noticed that one of the three or four pairs of pants he was wearing was down around his ankles. *That's strange,* I thought. We both got out of the car on that bitter cold Sunday morning in January and approached the man.

Looking at this man's face sent chills down my spine. It was as if I were looking at a marble statue. There was absolutely no movement, no expression, absolutely nothing. His face was drawn tight. His eyes were wide open but not in a responsive way. On the contrary, his eyes were fixed with that all-too-familiar thousand-yard stare, and for good reason. Sometime during the night this man had literally frozen to death.

Next to the man was a box of doughnuts that still had the receipt taped to it. According to the receipt, the doughnuts had been purchased just the day before. It was as if he had bought the doughnuts in anticipation of Sunday morning breakfast, a morning and a breakfast he would not live to see.

Homicide investigators were called to the scene, as was the local funeral home. The killer in this case was identified as Mother Nature. The frozen corpse was placed in the funeral home's station wagon and taken away.

This is America, I thought. *How in the world could a man sitting in a chair twenty feet from one of the busiest streets in town freeze to death?* I mean, somebody had to have seen this man. Surely someone had realized that the weather was bitterly cold that night.

In fact, it was deathly cold. As perhaps were the hearts of those who saw this man and continued on about their business.

Lesson 36: If we do not help, who will?

LESSON 37
WALKING WITH JESUS

Blessed are the people who know the joyful sound! They walk, O LORD, in the light of Your countenance.

—Psalm 89:15

I had seen the stranger from time to time, pushing the same old shopping cart. Judging from his appearance, it was obvious that he was homeless. The three or four layers of clothes he wore daily, and the fact that his face and black-and-gray beard were often covered with dirt were dead giveaways that like so many others in that area, his home was under the stars.

"Hey, how are you?" I would ask the man, but I didn't receive as much as a glance, let alone an answer. One day I tried to offer him a couple of dollars. He didn't accept. I eventually learned that the only way I could help the man was to give the cashier at the local convenience store a couple of dollars and tell her it was for the "homeless guy." She knew whom I was referring to.

In time we began to speak in passing, which was a major step as far as I was concerned. I learned that the man's name was Clarence Carter. He was in his sixties and had been living on the streets for several years. Clarence carried all his earthly possessions in a shopping cart that accompanied him everywhere he went. One day I noticed him limping badly as he pushed his shopping cart down the street.

"Mr. Carter, what's wrong with your leg?" I asked.

"I'm having problems with my feet again," he answered. "I'll be seeing the doctor about them next week."

"I tell you, Mr. Carter, I know of another man who may have had serious problems with his feet, considering all the walking he did," I said, realizing that I had a chance to bring up Jesus Christ.

"Who's that?"

"A man by the name of Jesus. Do you know him?" I asked.

Clarence began to smile. "Yeah, I know Him. I've been walking with him for a long, long time."

As I looked into the eyes of this street-hardened man, I suddenly noticed a peace that seemed to defy logic. Despite the toughness of his outward appearance, I realized that I was looking into the eyes of a true diamond in the rough. Clarence went on to share with me his love for and trust in Jesus Christ.

It really did my heart good, knowing that Clarence Carter, a picture of hopelessness and despair to the world, was actually a child of almighty God. True, he may have been homeless in the world's eyes, but in his heavenly Father's eyes he had a home, a home with the King of Kings and Lord of Lords.

I never looked at Clarence Carter the same again. I continued to see him pushing the same old grocery cart wearing the same old clothes for days, weeks, even months at a time, but I no longer saw a homeless man to be pitied. Instead I saw a stranger to this place, an alien to this world, a brother in Christ who like myself was just passing through this thing called life on the way toward his eternal home, sweet home.

It had been a couple of months since I had last spoken with Clarence when I received the tragic news. Clarence Carter, my friend and my brother in the Lord, had been found dead in a field. I found out later he had been beaten severely before being doused with gasoline and set on fire.

Clarence has finally gone home. The men responsible may think they ended Clarence's life. No, they didn't end it. They just made Clarence's walk with Jesus closer and sweeter than it had ever been on earth.

In a strange sort of way, Clarence's life has gone on uninterrupted. He walked with Jesus when the streets of this world were his home. He was walking with Jesus the night of his murder. And now he continues to walk with Jesus, his faithful companion throughout a life of hardships. I can't help but think there is one big difference … Clarence's walk with Jesus is no longer being done on the trash-strewn streets of the inner city, but rather on heaven's precious streets of gold.

Clarence, my friend, until we meet again on the other side, goodbye.

Lesson 37: If we want to walk with Jesus on the golden streets of heaven, we had better begin to do so on the uncertain streets of earth.

LESSON 38
IT'S A SMALL WORLD

Therefore judge nothing before the time, until the Lord comes, who will both bring to light the hidden things of darkness and reveal the counsels of the hearts. Then each one's praise will come from God.

—1 Corinthians 4:5

We watched from the shadows as the three men made a drug deal. Once finished, the three immediately began to disperse, the dealer with his money and the buyers with their drugs. Within seconds, four policemen on bicycles swooped down on the unsuspecting men like a hawk on its prey.

"Gun!" an officer shouted as he pressed the dealer up against a chain-link fence.

A police officer's life often depends on the ability to communicate with his partner as quickly and clearly as possible. When an officer shouts "Gun," it means just that: he sees a gun. In this case the officer had found a gun on the dealer.

Our response escalates from "Hey, man, what are you doing?" to "Get on the ground, now!"

Such was the case that night as all three men were quickly placed on the ground until they could each be searched for weapons. Once that threat was removed, the three men were helped to their feet before we questioned them about their activities in the area.

"It's like this, Randy," I began to explain to the suspected drug user I had stopped. "You are in the heart of cocaine country with a man who's carrying a gun at two thirty in the morning. My question is, why?"

Randy gave excuse after excuse, none of which were supported by his buddy, who was busy making up stories of his own.

"Do you have a picture ID, Randy?" I asked.

"No, sir," Randy answered.

"Do you have anything with your name on it to verify who you really are?"

"My name is Randy, sir. I'm not going to lie."

His name could be Randy, but then again it could be Larry or Darren or Tracy, I thought. I've come across many a man who, while standing in the middle of a blizzard, would swear it wasn't snowing. I learned early on as a police officer that truthfulness and the streets weren't exactly a peanut-butter-and-jelly or eggs-and-bacon kind of combination. For every reason I could give a person to tell the truth, he could give me a hundred reasons to lie.

"Randy, is there somebody I can call to verify who you are?"

Randy began to dig through his wallet when a light bulb seemed to go on. His look of worry and concern gave way to relief.

"What are you doing?" I couldn't help but ask.

"Officer Amos, I've got the name and number of my boss," Randy answered, obviously relieved that he had thought of such a plan.

"Randy, I hate to be the bearer of bad news, but it's almost three o'clock in the morning, and I doubt your boss is awake, and I imagine the place where you work is closed."

Randy's bubble began to deflate as he pulled the business card from his wallet.

I reached out for the card, figuring it couldn't hurt to see where Randy worked. I could always check with his boss later. I looked down at the card, where in disbelief I saw the name of Randy's boss, Elmer C. Baggott. I called my partner over to me.

"Dave, take a look at this," I said, handing the business card over to him.

"A business card for a guy named Baggott. So what." Dave appeared unimpressed by my discovery.

I pulled Dave to the side. "Randy the drug addict works for Elmer Baggott, my father-in-law!"

Dave began to laugh before asking, "Does Randy know he works for your father-in-law?"

"What do you think?" I answered.

"Does your father-in-law know he employs drug addicts?" Dave asked.

"Oh, give me about five hours and he will know," I said before turning and walking back over to Randy.

"So, Randy, who is this Baggott guy?" I asked.

"My boss man," Randy answered.

"Tell me, what's he like to work for?" I asked, figuring it's not every day that you get to hear what a complete stranger thinks of your father-in-law.

Lesson 38: When you stand before God, whose name will appear on your business card as boss man? "Jesus Christ," "Satan," or "self-employed"?

LESSON 39
"CAN I HAVE A LIFT?"

Sever yourselves from such a man, whose breath is in his nostrils; for of what account is he?

—Isaiah 2:22

My heart was racing and my palms were sweaty as I instructed the driver to get out of his car. *This is it,* I thought. *My first DUI arrest—don't blow it!* My field-training officer stood by, waiting for me to instruct the driver what to do. Once out of the car, I began to explain to the driver why I had stopped him and the purpose of the Standard Field Sobriety Test.

"Now, Mr. Williams, I am going to explain to you how to do the Field Sobriety Test. Do you understand?" I asked.

"Yes, sir," he answered nervously.

"The tests are nothing more than a tool to help me determine if you are driving under the influence."

I spent the next several minutes explaining and demonstrating each individual test. No sooner had I finished than two cars raced past us at a high rate of speed. I turned toward my training officer only to see that in the excitement of the moment, he had jumped in our police car and taken off like a missile in pursuit of the racing cars.

Okay, Chris, now what? I asked myself as the siren from our police car grew fainter and fainter before fading out altogether in the distance.

Stay calm, Chris. I know we never covered this in the police academy, but look on the bright side: Williams doesn't know that.

"Okay, sir, as I was saying, the first test I need you to do is the heel-to-toe test." I had rehearsed this speech a million times before, waiting for my big chance to use it in a real-life scenario. Unfortunately, my rehearsed speech was being seriously hampered by the police radio traffic involving the pursuit my training officer was in.

It's no use, I thought. *I can't talk, walk, and listen all at the same time.* I stopped giving instructions to Mr. Williams, and the two of us began to listen intently to my radio as my training officer gave out the speeds and directions of travel of the two cars he was chasing. Almost as quickly as the pursuit began, it ended in a multiple-car accident about twenty blocks away.

A thought suddenly dawned on me. *Chris, your partner is twenty blocks away involved in an accident, and here you are, stranded in a poorly lit parking lot with a borderline drunk driver. Now what?*

"Mr. Williams," I began, "it seems we are both in a bit of a dilemma. You've been stopped for possibly driving under the influence of alcohol, and I'm stranded."

Mr. Williams gave a halfhearted smile as he shook his head in agreement.

"I have an idea," I continued. "It's called a road test and works like this. If you are willing to give me a lift to where my partner is, I will have the opportunity to observe your driving ability. If we get there in one piece, I will use what they call an 'officer's discretion' and give you a break. Agreed?"

"Sounds good to me, sir," Mr. Williams answered, more than a little surprised.

We pulled up to the scene of the accident. I thanked Mr. Williams for the lift and instructed him not to drink and drive in the future. He assured me he would not. I found my training officer standing next to the totaled stolen car he had been chasing.

"Hey, A.J., are you okay?" I asked.

A.J. looked up with a puzzled look on his face, obviously not expecting to see me. "How did you get here?"

"Well, remember the borderline drunk?"

"Yeah, what about him?"

"I asked him to give me a ride."

A.J. shook his head in disbelief as I pointed to the car that had just dropped me off.

"You're crazy," A.J. responded.

"Yeah, you and me both, A.J. You and me both."

Lesson 39: Never put yourself in a position where you look to the world to bail you out.

LESSON 40
MATTHEW

The last enemy that will be destroyed is death.

—1 Corinthians 15:26

Every officer will see one sooner or later in his or her career. Some look forward to the occasion as a time of learning, whereas others dread the day. Most will stand by watching quietly, not wanting to let anyone around know that they are disturbed in the slightest by the experience. Once finished, officers usually begin with the jokes. I learned long ago that the number one mechanism used by police officers to get through day after day of dealing with pain, suffering, and death is to simply joke about it. Does it work? It never did for me.

I will never forget my first time. I walked down a long, narrow hallway to a door that was tightly shut. A man wearing a white lab coat turned toward me and asked, "Are you ready?" I nodded and the door swung open. I walked into the room and sensed a coldness that sent chills down my spine.

I looked around, surprised by the blandness of the large rectangular room I had entered. No thousand-dollar instruments. No state-of-the-art medical machines. None of the annoying beeps and buzzes one grows accustomed to hearing in a medical facility. Nothing even close to what I had expected. In fact, the tools and instruments that I saw on the countertops and hanging from the walls reminded me more of my own garage than a state medical examiner's lab. The closer I looked, the more I realized that just about everything was metal. The tools, instruments, trays, countertops, sink basins, and even the large table at the far end of the room were all made of stainless steel. This gave an appearance that was cold and callous.

I noticed a hose running from one of the sinks to the large metal table. A couple of people were leaning over the table as I slowly began to make my way toward that end of the room.

"Good morning, Officer Amos," a woman welcomed me as I approached the table.

"Good morning, ma'am."

"Is this your first autopsy?" she asked.

Apparently from the expression on my face, it was a question that didn't have to be asked, but she did so just the same.

"Yes, it is."

"Well, I am Dr. Hightower, one of Virginia's state medical examiners. In a nutshell, my job is to try to determine the cause of death in homicides and other cases where the exact cause is unknown."

"Sounds like a great job," I said sarcastically.

"Oh, it has its benefits," Dr. Hightower answered before explaining to me just how the victim she was currently working on had died. "Tragic death—yes, a very tragic death. The victim, Officer Amos, was named Matthew." Dr. Hightower paused for a second. "He was only five years old. Matthew was fatally beaten by his mother's boyfriend." She went on to describe the beating in detail.

I watched the autopsy, unable to believe that what I was watching was an actual human being. *Chris,* I told myself, *that can't be a little boy.* As I watched Dr. Hightower and her assistant conduct their examination, I tried to convince myself that the small child was really just a side of beef. *Yeah, that's it, Chris,* I told myself. *It's just a side of beef.*

As the examination was winding down, I began to breathe a sigh of relief. *A tragic death indeed,* I thought as I was preparing to leave. Suddenly the "side of beef" that I had been watching became a precious, innocent little five-year-old boy who had died a terrible and senseless death.

At the end of the autopsy Matthew's face was pulled back down over what had been just an indistinguishable skull. The "side of beef" I had been watching now had soft lips that should have been singing "Jesus Loves Me," tiny eyes that should have been opening wide with excitement at the sight of cotton candy, and a freckle-covered nose that should have been straining to smell the flowers in Grandma's garden.

Like a dam breaking and being washed aside by thousands of gallons of rushing water, my defensive mechanism was shattered. I left that room feeling as though I were leaving a little piece of myself with Matthew.

The sight of little Matthew's face haunted me for several weeks. My hatred for sin grew as I came face-to-face with yet another one of Satan's masterpieces: child abuse. In spite of my anger, I gained comfort in knowing Matthew was in a better place, a place that knew nothing of pain and suffering, of child abuse and death, a place where Matthew is receiving that which he had not here: love, unconditional and beyond measure.

Lesson 40: The portrait of pain and suffering Satan is painting will one day be wiped clean with one stroke by the Master. God is the Master, and the blood of Jesus Christ is the stroke.

LESSON 41
A LEGACY OF LOVE

And we have known and believed the love that God has
for us. God is love, and he who abides in love abides in
God, and God in him.

—1 John 4:16

The words cut to the very core of my heart as I knelt beside my six-
year-old son, Seth, listening as he said his good-night prayers.

"God, thank you for Mommy and Daddy and Jesse and Hannah.
And God, please help my daddy not get killed at work."

I assured Seth that my guardian angel was watching out for me
before tucking him in and kissing him good night. I spent the better
part of that night wondering why Seth had said that. Had something
happened at work to trigger his prayer? I had made it a point never to
talk about close calls around our kids. In fact, I tried not to talk about
them, period. Why would he say such a thing?

Oh, I've been asked a thousand times if I worried about being shot
or stabbed. What police officer hasn't? But this was different. It's one
thing to be asked by a complete stranger; it's quite another when the one
asking is your own son, your baby. I would usually blow the question
off by simply answering "no" or "Hey, death is a promotion." I would
not be able to escape Seth's words quite that easily.

I began to ask myself that dreaded question: *Chris, what if you were killed at work?* How would Anne Marie cope? What about Seth and Jesse? Both are daddy's boys through and through—at least they are if you ask their daddy. And then there was Hannah, my one-year-old angel. How would she ever get to know her daddy? I've seen life after life come to a sudden, unexpected, often violent end. Who's to say the same will not happen to me?

The more I thought, the more I began to sense the presence of the Holy Spirit. I began to sense a peace that for a few minutes had been overwhelmed with anxiety and uncertainty.

Life is unpredictable at best. Each day I am given to spend with my family is just that: a gift given with no guarantee that another will follow. My job as a husband and a father is to make the most of each and every one, fleshing out the love, integrity, and consistency of a man wholly devoted to his Savior and Lord Jesus Christ, to his family, and to his church. I have failed to do this at times, and yet in God's grace, He has given me yet another day to do better.

If I am killed at work today, I will stand before Jesus knowing that Anne Marie, Seth, Jesse, and Hannah had, in me, a husband and father who truly lived life striving to obediently flesh out the love of Jesus Christ. I've taken the necessary steps to see to it that my family is taken care of financially, as most folks have. But I know that if this is to be my last day on the streets of Norfolk, I have given my family a gift far greater in value, a peace and assurance that their husband and daddy will be standing at the entrance of heaven, waiting eagerly for that eternal reunion with his wife and kids, never to be separated again by death, forever and ever.

Lesson 41: The greatest gift a person can leave his or her family is the hope of an eternal reunion in heaven. Have you given this gift to your family?

LESSON 42
"OFFICER DOWN!"

Yea, though I walk through the valley of the shadow of death, I will fear no evil; For You are with me; Your rod and Your staff, they comfort me.

—Psalm 23:4

My partner Dave Huffman keyed his police radio. "Clear the air! One-six-two [my call sign] and one-six-three [Huffman's call sign] are in pursuit in the 1400 block of Corprew." The dispatcher turned the channel over to us as we began chasing two men, both of whom were engaged in a drug deal when the pursuit began. The two men split up, each running in a different direction. Dave and I did likewise, each chasing a different suspect. We were both on twenty-one-speed mountain bikes, so within a matter of seconds I had caught up to the man I was pursuing.

"Give it up, man! Just give it up!" I shouted at the man, who was wearing a dark-colored jacket, blue jeans, and black tennis shoes. I was within four feet of the man, preparing to knock him to the ground, when my life changed forever.

"Shots fired! I've got shots fired!" Dave shouted over the radio, a sense of urgency in his voice. "Chris, where are you?" An eerie silence followed. "Chris, where are you?" There was still no answer.

143

Suddenly, the silence was broken. "One-six-two," I managed to get out, trying to stay as calm and levelheaded as possible. "I've been hit. I've been hit."

While lying in a hospital bed later that night, I had a chance to relive the eight seconds on Bond Street that has forever changed my life.

The suspect had continued to run from me despite my attempts to get him to give up. Realizing I would have to physically take this guy into custody, I was preparing to do so. In fact, I was within a second or two of tackling the suspect when without warning, he jerked back toward me. It was a dark street, so I could not see the gun in his right hand. Suddenly the darkness was interrupted by a flash of light and an ear-piercing bang. Immediately I felt a thud to the right side of my chest.

The impact of that first round into my chest was like a well-placed blow with a hammer. Thank God I was wearing my bulletproof vest when I needed it most. My initial reaction was to squeeze the brakes on my bike. The bike stopped, but I did not, and I went sailing up and over the handlebars. While I was in the air, a second flash of light and ear-splitting bang occurred. This round ripped through the thigh of my left leg. An excruciating pain raced throughout my body as I fell to the ground, bleeding and dazed. I covered my head, anticipating three, four, or five more rounds to tear through my body. I lay motionless, not moving a muscle, not making a sound, preparing on that cold city street to enter the Valley of Death.

"Chris," the still, gentle voice said, "Get behind Me," and with that, it was as if the Good Shepherd Himself, Jesus Christ, had come to rescue one of His fallen sheep. Before I knew it, I had rolled onto my side, with the bulk of my weight resting squarely on my bleeding thigh. The suspect had turned to run away. He had gotten about ten yards when, to his surprise, he saw me move. I imagine he thought I was dead after having shot me twice from less than five feet away. Realizing I was still alive, he had immediately turned back and raised his gun again to finish what he had begun. My gun was drawn by this time and there we were, ten yards apart, each pointing a gun at the other. We fired simultaneously. My entire body tightened as I expected to be hit again. A second passed, then another and another as I anticipated where his next round would hit. *He missed. He actually missed,* I thought, as a strange kind of relief swept over my body. He was not as fortunate. My round struck him in the chest. I fired two more times, one of which struck him in the head. I was told the nineteen-year-old suspect died instantly. In one hand he held the gun he had used to try to kill me. In the other was a wad of dollar bills. Back at the scene where the pursuit began, $150.00 worth of marijuana was recovered. This man had died as he had lived, surrounded by drugs, guns, and cash.

Seconds after he had fired the first shot, the incident was over. Just that quick, one life had ended and another had been permanently changed. Two men were on the street that night. One had God and the other did not.

I received God's unearned grace, mercy, and miraculous deliverance. The suspect received God's holy wrath and judgment. In a sense, that evening was just a taste of what is to come for all who have rejected Jesus. There will be a great separation between the Lord's sheep and the wolves that prey upon them. In a day and age when society has lost all fear of God, I witnessed a holy wrath that rekindled a healthy, reverent fear for almighty God. He truly is worthy of all our praise and worship, but not at the expense of a holy, righteous, reverential fear from saint and sinner alike.

There are those who believe that Christianity is for old ladies and children. That it has no bearing on a person's real life. Friend, I can attest to the fact that Christianity is also for a police officer fighting for his very life while lying on a cold, dark city street. It's been said that God meets those who simply trust in Him at their point of need. Seven years earlier my point of need was as a sinner who had lost all hope, sitting on the end of his bed preparing to commit suicide. The Lord met me then with three words that saved my life: "There is hope." On this night, my point of need was that of a wounded lamb in need of rescue. The Lord met me once again as He spoke the words that once again saved my life: "Chris, get behind me." God delivered both times as He has done countless times before and since.

I have been told that what happened was the by-product of good training. Well-wishers from all over the country as well as Canada and England have told me how proud they were of the way I handled myself.

In fact, many have gone as far as to call me a hero. Three nights after the shooting I was alone in my bedroom, remembering the kind words of so many. I asked God to protect me from self-pride. In response to my request, God began to overwhelm me with His love to an extent that I had never experienced in my life. "God, stop!" I begged, gasping for air as I wept uncontrollably. "Please stop. You are killing me with your love, Father. Please ... please stop." And yet it was while drowning in this divine love that God allowed me to see my part in the shooting three nights earlier.

I had hit the ground wounded and dazed but still levelheaded enough to respond. Immediately, my training had kicked in, and I had begun to slow my breathing so as to make a smoother and more accurate shot. Once my breathing had become more manageable, I had rolled onto my side. Within seconds, my weapon had been drawn. I had reached across my body, holding my gun with one hand. I had waited patiently until I had the suspect squarely in my sights, and began to squeeze the trigger in a smooth, precise manner, not concerned with the weapon pointed back at ... *not!* No, on the contrary, my actions weren't those of a well-trained, well-prepared police officer reacting instinctively to the threat of danger. No, a much better description of my actions would be that of a spiritual infant clinging desperately to his heavenly Father for dear life. I trusted in God at the most crucial point of need imaginable and He delivered!

My wife, Anne Marie, has an interesting theory about the third bullet that the suspect fired at me from ten yards away. The bullet was never recovered by the police crime scene investigators. Anne Marie thinks that when I get to heaven and run up to Jesus to give Him a great big hug, He will lift up His arm and hold out His hand. As I draw closer, He will open His palm, and there in the palm of the King of kings and Lord of Lords will be that third bullet. I can almost hear Him ask, "Were you worried about this, my son? Didn't you know I was in control? I had it all the time, my child. I had it all the time. I was in control."

What about you? What situation or circumstance are you worried about? Maybe it is a broken relationship, a wayward son or daughter, mother or father, husband or wife. Maybe you're facing a sickness or a financial burden too great to handle. What is it that Jesus Christ will hold up to you and say, "Were you worried about him or her, this or that, my child? I had him, I had her, all the time. Didn't you know I was in control?"

Lesson 42: In a world of "Goliaths" bent on killing and destroying those who call themselves Christians, praise the Lord! The God of David still holds the sling.

Angels in Blue
for Seth, Jesse and Hannah
by Anne Marie Amos

We must not forget to thank our Lord
for police officers on the street.
For they work in a world with little respect
and have many duties to meet.
Hoping for each day, justice and peace
to prevail over lawless foe,
Our officers put their lives on the line
to protect and serve, we all know.
Not too long ago, my dad and his partner
were responding in pursuit
Of two lawless men who were dealing drugs;
they split up, our officers, too.
As drugs were recovered with his partner's win,
my dad was closing on prey.
In the blink of an eye, my daddy was shot
in the chest and in the leg.
As he fell to the ground expecting more shots,
he received complete help from above.
As he lifted his arms and had sights on his foe,
he squeezed the gun in his glove.
At the very same time, the foe shot again,
hoping my dad would just die.

If he'd only just known what I knew from the start,
my dad serves the living Christ.
The bullet my dad shot went straight to foe's chest,
the second one to foe's head.
The last bullet the foe shot at my dad
has yet to be found, so is said.
My dad is recovering now from the wound
inflicted while doing his job.
His partner's now looking for other foe
and is caring for Dad and us all.
Now, I not only thank the Lord
for police officers on the street.
I thank the Lord for protecting their lives
and the victories of which they speak.
Next time you kneel and say your prayers,
I ask this request of you:
Please don't forget to thank the Lord
for police officers, our *Angels in Blue*.

LESSON 43
FINAL EXAM

> I planted, Apollos watered, but God gave the increase. So then neither he who plants is anything, nor he who waters, but God who gives the increase. Now he who plants and he who waters are one, and each one will receive his own reward according to his own labor. For we are God's fellow workers; you are God's field, you are God's building.
>
> —1 Corinthians 3:6–9

After reading the lessons contained within this book, one might think that this guy Amos is some kind of a "S-U-P-E-R- C-H-R-I-S-T-I-A-N!"

Faster than the fiery arrows of Satan, stronger than the strongest demonic stronghold, able to win the world to Christ any time, any place, any day with a single prayer. Well, you get the idea. I've got a confession to make. Just between you and me, there has been many a day when I have felt like anything but a fruitful child of almighty God.

Within these pages you have read of many men and women with whom I have shared the Good News of Jesus Christ, and yet these experiences have not been without opposition—opposition that has often taken the wind right out of my witnessing sails. Oh, how I have wrestled with the idea that many of those to whom I speak experience the classic "foxhole" conversion, which is quickly forgotten or out-and-out abandoned once the trial has passed. I have struggled with feelings of guilt that arise out of my inability to do more for the men and women with whom I share. I mean, I witness and pray, and then I go my way as they go theirs. Unfortunately, their way more times than not is back into an environment or situation that is usually contrary to the will and way of Jesus Christ. And then there are those opportunities that, to be perfectly honest, I have willfully chosen not to take advantage of because I was hungry or tired or cold or wet or scared or embarrassed or … you get the idea.

I find that the enemy often attempts to use these missed opportunities, as well as the accompanying disheartening thoughts, to steal the very joy and peace God has given me. Fortunately, a loving and gracious heavenly Father never ceases to amaze as He faithfully reminds me of an earlier lesson learned: "Remember Satan's favorite weapon, the lie."

Christians, I challenge each and every one of you to begin praying today, if you aren't already, for God to bring folks into your life who desperately need to hear what you and I have to say. The world promotes the "one-night stand" as something to be had by all, a great time without the commitment.

Guess what? Our heavenly Father encourages His own version of the "one-night stand." Unlike the world's version, God's is done not for what a person can get, but rather for what he or she can give. You see, there are countless numbers of Marys and Floyds, Alberts, Jeffs, and Tonys out there whom we will encounter only once, in a "one-night stand," so to speak. When these encounters occur, and they will, we have the opportunity to give them the most precious gift we possess, the Good News of Jesus Christ. I promise that if we obediently share that gift, God has in store for us lessons that when learned will revolutionize our walk with Him.

Lesson 43: God's will is that we simply share the Good News and leave the saving to Him. God is in need of fewer soul winners and more seed planters.

Master Police Officer **Chris Amos** is a twenty-four-year veteran of the Norfolk Police Department. A Medal of Valor and Life Saving recipient, Chris is currently the department's spokesman. Chris pastors Calvary Temple Church in Norfolk, Virginia. He has spoken at churches and conferences throughout the country, appeared on the 700 Club, and had his testimony dramatized on the radio program "Unshackled!" Chris and his wife, Anne Marie, have three children and live in Norfolk, Virginia.

Chris Amos is available for speaking engagements. He can be contacted at cop4god@gmail.com.